OPERATION
RESCUE
A Challenge to the
Nation's Conscience

OPERATION RESCUE

A Challenge to the Nation's Conscience

Philip F. Lawler

Our Sunday Visitor Publishing Division
Our Sunday Visitor, Inc.
Huntington, Indiana 46750

For all the babies we fail to save.

CONTENTS

Prologue: A Sidewalk Drama

IN THE predawn darkness we barely recognize one another. Most of us have come with a few friends. We stay huddled together with them now, close to our cars, talking quietly, shuffling and stamping our feet to keep warm. Several hours from now, the parking lot at this busy suburban shopping center will be packed with cars; the air will be tinged with exhaust fumes. But at five A.M. the lot is deserted, and the only "exhaust" comes in the clouds of frozen breath that arise from our small knots of conversation. The yawning acres of empty asphalt all around us are quiet. And cold.

We aren't always this quiet. Back on Thursday evening we raised the roof of a nearby church with our foot-stomping hymns. Our prayers were loud and fervent that night. They were fervent earlier this morning, too, when we gathered for four-A.M. worship services: Mass for the Catholics, a prayer service for Protestants. The fervor stays with us still, beneath a layer of quiet anticipation. We mingle with others in the crowd, nodding to friends, hearing an occasional nervous laugh, and we wait.

Now headlights flicker across the black, and two compact cars arrive on the fringe of our little encampment. A handful of newcomers — unrecognizable at this distance — emerge and fan out through the crowd, passing the message: "We're ready. Everybody back in your cars. Let's go!" Three dozen motors kick into action.

Near the mall entrance, two men stand shivering, one on each side of the road. They stop each car, looking for a familiar face, asking for a reference; then, when they are satisfied, they hand out maps and instructions. We're off!

Our caravan rolls down the highway intact. There is virtually no traffic so early on Saturday morning, and as we ride along in solitude, the still air exaggerates the sensation of speed. The instructions are clear enough, but the destination is unfamiliar, so we carefully follow the taillights ahead, checking our rearview mirror constantly. The front of the convoy is already out of sight ahead of us, the rear still several cars behind.

We reach the city along with the first rays of light. We meet some light traffic on the main streets, and our directions call for several quick turns. Since stoplights have split up the motorcade, we concentrate on the maps. After a few tricky intersections we arrive at the site, pull over, and park. Our leaders have already arrived; a few dozen people are clustered at the doors of a squat, nondescript brick building. As we join the crowd, two young women break off, carrying a long banner, and unfurl it at the curb. They stand silently facing the westbound traffic, illuminated by the eerie colors of dawn, so that curious motorists can read the message: "Operation Rescue in Progress."

* * *

No one expected us here. The building is empty. The abortionist's first appointment is two hours away. Before anyone notices us (aside from the early-morning passersby, who stop to stare, then continue on their way), we have set up our blockade. Approximately fifty people sit tightly packed in front of the main entrance; perhaps another thirty guard the rear door. Once again, there is nothing to do but wait and pray. Someone has passed out mimeographed sheets of hymns, and we begin to sing. Occasionally the leaders interrupt to issue some instructions, and then the singing resumes.

Four pro-abortion activists — two women, two men — have arrived with us. Somehow they cadged a map, or perhaps they simply followed us into the city. Once we have settled into our position at the doors, they jump up from within our ranks, and begin shouting slogans. We have been trained to ignore them, and we do. But they persist, angrily shouting even louder, striving to drown out our hymns and prayers. Frustrated, they shove their way out of our midst, but they continue screaming insults from the fringe. We can't help but wonder: Where do these poor people find the energy to continue — to keep on shouting — when no one is paying attention?

Finally a police cruiser arrives. The officer surveys the scene, clearly confused by what he sees. He pulls aside our leader, and talks for a few minutes, shaking his head repeatedly. He returns to his car and makes a radio call. Again he speaks briefly with our leader. Again he returns to his vehicle. And he leaves! A cheer goes up from our ranks, but the leaders quickly wave their hands for quiet. The police will be back.

A middle-aged woman arrives next: apparently one of the clinic's employees. She strides purposefully toward the rear door, her jaw set, her blue eyes cold. We stand and link arms, blocking her progress. She stands still for a few moments, arms akimbo, then whirls and stalks back to her car. In a few moments two police cars pull up, and she confronts them immediately, demanding that they clear her path.

The police lieutenant addresses us. "You have a right to demonstrate," he says, "but not to block the door. You must move."

No one moves.

"If you do not leave," he warns us, "you will be subject to arrest."

No one moves.

Two more police cruisers have arrived, and another woman who works at the abortion clinic. The lieutenant has conferred with someone on his radio. The clinic's first customer has arrived, too: a small, pretty young woman, perhaps twenty years old, giggling mirthlessly at the commotion. Under the lieutenant's instruction the police form a phalanx, with two burly officers at the front, the three women close behind them, and two more police bringing up the rear. The lieutenant issues another warning: If we do not move, they will clear a path forcibly.

No one moves.

The first assault comes at the rear entry. The police start against the wall, trying to wedge their way to the door. In the front ranks of the blockade, people are still seated. The police shove them aside and step over or around them, with the clinic workers still close behind them. But whenever a gap appears, someone else scoots over to fill the space. The police mutter a few curses and call in a few reinforcements.

Soon bodies are flying everywhere. The Rescuers closest to the door stand and lock arms again. But in the front of the blockade our friends are pinned to their places on the ground, with the police stepping over them, reaching down to pick up other Rescuers and toss them on top of the pile. We hear grunts, a few angry shouts, more curses — and through it all, the strong, prayerful voices from the front entry to the clinic, still singing hymns.

One tall policeman has fought his way through the seated Rescuers to within just six feet of the door. Now he grabs the last standing Rescuers, one by one, and hurls them headlong away from the door, back down the narrow corridor he and his partners have created. But as soon as one Rescuer goes careening down that path, another steps into his place near the door. And when a Rescuer is tossed away from the door on one side — stumbling, often ricocheting off the brick wall — he promptly circles around the blockade, to rejoin it from the other side. The entire crowd moves like an amoeba, filling up the space beside the wall, guarding the door. Despite all their exertions, the police are making no further progress toward the door. Eventually they stop, throw up their hands, and look back toward the lieutenant for instructions. For two or three minutes everyone is frozen in place. Then reluctantly the lieutenant signals his men to retreat, and the first assault is over.

On an ordinary day the clinic would be open by now, and that first young woman would be in the abortion chamber. The two clinic workers complain bitterly to the police, then adjourn to the parking lot, where they stand near their cars sipping coffee throughout the morning, returning to renew their complaints periodically.

Left by herself, the young woman who came to seek an abortion this morning heads back to her own car. But two other young women approach her. One is dressed in black, with a "Pro-Choice" button on her leather jacket. The other wears a bright red sweater and carries a handful of pro-life pamphlets. At first the troubled young woman waves away the pro-life counselor, bursting into tears on the other woman's shoulder. After several minutes, however, she wipes her eyes, and when the pro-life worker returns, she agrees to look at a pamphlet that describes the development of her unborn child. The black-clad woman protests angrily, snatches the pamphlet and shreds it. But the pro-life counselor offers another copy; the young woman takes it. They strike up a conversation, and soon the two women leave the scene together, headed for breakfast at a local coffee shop. Before the end of the day the pregnant woman will decide to cancel her scheduled abortion, continue her pregnancy, and keep the baby. Operation Rescue has its first "save" of the day.

Back at the clinic doors, few people have seen this vital drama unfold. But we have been praying as the stalemate continues and busloads of police reinforcements arrive — praying for the lives of unborn children. As the morning wears on, several new police commanders arrive, and each one pleads with us to leave off our blockade. Speaking through a bullhorn, one captain tries to explain the situation with exaggerated patience. "You have made your demonstration," he begins.

From somewhere in our midst, a lone exasperated voice shouts in reply: *"This is not a demonstration!"*

By midmorning the police have brought in enough manpower to begin the laborious process of arresting everyone involved in the blockade. After one final warning, they wade into the crowd, picking up Rescuers one by one, dragging or carrying them to a waiting bus. When the bus is full — ending a time-consuming process, since every Rescuer collapses into a limp posture when the police grab him — the driver climbs behind the steering wheel, then shakes his head in dismay. A dozen Rescuers are sitting on the street, blocking his path. The painstaking process of arrest begins anew. Another hour has passed before the police finally clear the path to the clinic's rear door. An ardent group of pro-abortion activists, gathered by now at the site, jeer as each busload of Rescuers heads off to the local jail. They cheer wildly when the clinic doors open, but their cheers are misplaced. It is nearly noon, and all of the day's abortions were scheduled for earlier this morning. One worker enters the clinic with a triumphant flourish, but the abortionist himself never bothers. He has no work to do.

Nor do the police bother to break up the blockade outside the front door. Instead they negotiate a compromise with the remaining Rescuers. In exchange for a promise that no abortions will take place today, the Rescuers end their blockade. They will remain on the sidewalk for another hour, prayerful and vigilant.

The police claim victory because the clinic doors were opened. The clinic workers claim victory because they won access to their office. The pro-abortion activists outside claim victory because, by the time eighty Rescuers have been carted off to jail, the pro-abortion crowd outnumbers the remaining pro-lifers.

Operation Rescue claims victory because at this one place, on this one day, no unborn babies died.

1

A Movement Is Born

THE EARLY 1980s were a quiet time for America. As the
decade began, the nation was at peace; the economy was
growing; the tumultuous civic disturbances of the late 1960s
were fading into the history texts. Yet before the decade ended,
Americans witnessed two astonishing developments —
developments which could shape our country's history well into the
next millennium.

On the international scene, the Berlin Wall came crashing down,
and international Communism teetered toward its own sudden,
inexplicable collapse. On the domestic front, after simmering for a
full generation, the debate over abortion finally boiled over, and
activist groups took to the streets. For half a century, American
foreign policy had been dominated by our confrontation with a
seemingly irreconcilable adversary. Now that adversary
unexpectedly withdrew from the scene; the Cold War abruptly
ended. Even as they celebrated the demise of Communism, however,
Americans found themselves locked in an equally momentous
confrontation at home: a battle for control of American culture.
Public debates over homosexuality, pornography, abortion, and
euthanasia had revealed a fundamental split in our society; the two
contending parties disagree not only on *how* to pursue the good life,
but on what the good life *is*. Christianity, once the dominant moral
force guiding American society, had been reduced to the level of a
counterculture. Secular liberals not only ignore the precepts of
Judeo-Christian morality, but condemn that entire moral tradition as
unhealthy and oppressive. Here too, the conflict seems irreconcilable.

No public issue illustrates this fundamental conflict more clearly
than the debate over legalized abortion. And no movement captures
the abortion battle more vividly than Operation Rescue.

From the civil-rights campaign of the late 1960s, through the
peace demonstrations of the Vietnam era, and continuing with
environmental activism, Americans had grown accustomed to protest

movements and acts of civil disobedience. But when Operation Rescue (OR) burst into prominence in the late 1980s, most ordinary Americans were caught unprepared. This new movement shattered all the public expectations about civil disobedience. The people being carted off to jail were not members of some oppressed minority; they were from predominantly comfortable middle-class backgrounds. They were not career agitators; most had never faced a legal charge more serious than a traffic violation, and it would be difficult to find any group in American society with more respect for the police and the role of law. Perhaps most confusing, the OR activists were not radicals — at least not in the ordinary sense; the cause they served was a profoundly conservative one.

For those who examined the phenomenon a bit more carefully, OR offered yet another disconcerting surprise. This was not just one more pressure group agitating for political change, not simply the latest addition to the pro-life campaign. Linked together with its pro-life mission, OR also proclaimed a religious goal: the public revival of American Christianity. OR leaders claimed that their actions were not merely allowed, but actually required by their Christian moral obligations.

Was OR a new religious sect, offering some radical new innovation in Christian moral theology? Not at all. In fact, the moral insight that inspired Operation Rescue is as old as Christianity itself. Jesus Himself sacrificed His life to save guilty sinners. Couldn't His followers sacrifice their freedom — even just temporarily — to save the innocent?

In the earliest days of the Church, when Christians first turned their attention to the social problems of the late Roman Empire, the very first Christian political movement was a campaign to save babies. Under the Roman law of *paterfamilias*, a newborn baby had no rights whatsoever until formally embraced by the father. The father would stand before a special altar and raise the infant in his arms, proclaiming the baby as his own child. But if for any reason the father did not want that baby, he would abandon it at the foot of the altar, where the child would soon die of exposure or neglect. Christian leaders condemned that practice. Christian families defied the law by taking those abandoned children into their own homes.

And finally a prominent Christian activist named Basil went a step further, destroying that altar.

In a sense, then, Operation Rescue is nothing new. Christians like Basil were rescuing babies, in open defiance of the law, sixteen hundred years ago; today we honor them as saints. And their sacrifices paid dividends. In the year 374, the Emperor Valentinian outlawed infanticide, and the bloody pagan tradition of *paterfamilias* was dead.

Now flash forward across the centuries to the contemporary United States, where the law gives women a nearly absolute right to abort their unborn children. Call it *materfamilias*, if you will: a legal sanction to make life-or-death decisions as absolute and as arbitrary as those made by pagan men just before the fall of Rome. Again the Christian churches — especially the Roman Catholic — thundered condemnation of the slaughter, and Christian families reached out to save babies, offering housing, medical care, financial help, and adoption services for troubled pregnant women. Inevitably some activist would follow the example of Basil, and take the next step. When?

The first American "rescue" took place long before the Supreme Court's fateful *Roe v. Wade* decision. In September 1969, Federal Judge Gerhard Gesell ruled that the law prohibiting abortion in the District of Columbia was "unconstitutionally vague" and therefore invalid. Within weeks, the nation's capital city was home to the busiest abortion industry in the Eastern United States. (In California, Governor Ronald Reagan had signed the nation's most permissive abortion law two years earlier.) At the editorial offices of *Triumph*, a small, conservative Catholic magazine, editor Brent Bozell and his colleagues concluded that "someone must go beyond words. All we have left is action." After huddling with his staff and a few other Catholic friends, Bozell decided to arrange a "demonstration" on June 6, 1970.

Late in May, Bozell and his faithful remnant wrote to five Washington hospitals, asking them to curb their abortion business voluntarily on June 6, and warning that if they did not, "There will be Christians on hand to administer the baptism prior to the killings — if they cannot be prevented." Those letters went unanswered, and on June 6, a few hundred demonstrators marched from a morning

Mass to the doors of the George Washington University clinic. After a short rally, Bozell led a handful of young men past security guards and into the clinic, while the remaining demonstrators stood at the door praying the rosary.

This was 1970, remember. Richard Nixon was President; protests against the Vietnam War were near their peak, and Washington's police force had grown accustomed to dealing with political demonstrations forcefully. The police were puzzled by Bozell's little platoon, but not too puzzled to act. Using their nightsticks liberally, they promptly tossed two demonstrators out of the clinic and arrested five others. The demonstration quickly ended.

Triumph magazine had seen Bozell's "Action for Life" as a sign of "Catholics on the march in America." But in fact the little movement disappeared after that one episode. Eventually all five of the men arrested on June 6 were convicted on charges of unlawful entry; four were also found guilty of assault. One participant was summarily fired from his job as a congressional aide. Even *The Wanderer*, the most conservative of America's Catholic newspapers, denounced the Action for Life in a scalding editorial. *Triumph* folded, Bozell suffered an emotional breakdown, and his little band dispersed. There would be no repeat performances.

Roe v. Wade galvanized the pro-life movement, and countless thousands of Americans plunged into their first real political work. Committees were formed, money was raised, bills were introduced, rallies were organized, books were published, legislators were lobbied, letters were written — the outpouring of social activism from every conceivable approach. Every approach, that is, except direct action. No new organization arose to duplicate Action for Life.

In Tennessee, a young woman named Joan Andrews was appalled and bewildered by the absence of a public response. After months of prayer, she decided to begin her own private crusade. "I decided to go to Chicago to smash the abortion weapons," she writes:

> "I chose Chicago because it was close enough to get to easily but far enough away so that my parents would not necessarily hear about what I was doing and be worried. But the idea just did not jell. I went there, but I did not do much. After a while, I went home."

17

In fact, a concerned policeman found Joan Andrews on the streets early one morning, alone and seemingly bewildered. He helpfully guided her onto a bus back to her home in Tennessee. She did not "smash the abortion weapons." But from that moment on, she would later recall, Joan Andrews expected to spend the remainder of her life defying the laws that allowed legal abortion, probably shuttling in and out of jail, fighting to save unborn children.

Joan Andrews did not know it when she embarked on her solitary mission to Chicago, but she was not alone. A handful of dedicated pro-life activists, scattered all across the country, had begun to plan direct action to stop abortion. Right there in Chicago, the nation's best known pro-life activist, Joseph Scheidler, was already developing his repertory of techniques to stop the abortion industry: picketing, passing out literature on the sidewalks, calling press conferences to highlight the slaughter, passing out leaflets at clinics, marching inside to disrupt the business, showing photographs of aborted babies, rummaging through dumpsters to accumulate the grisly evidence of the slaughter, putting padlocks on clinic doors. Scheidler — a tall, physically imposing man with a booming voice — supplemented his fearless dedication with a lively tactical imagination. First near his own Chicago base, then gradually in concert with new-found allies in other regions, he developed more and more inventive ways to stall the abortion industry. Immediately recognizable because of his height, his beard, his hat, and his trademark bullhorn, Scheidler became Public Enemy Number One for abortionists all over the country. The title of his book, published in 1985, captures Scheidler's no-holds-barred approach: *Closed: 99 Ways to Stop Abortion.*

Scheidler was not alone; he was only the most visible pro-lifer who had chosen direct attempts to close abortion clinics, rather than more roundabout lobbying campaigns to change the law. In the early aftermath of *Roe v. Wade*, pro-lifers had very few channels of communication. At the annual conventions sponsored by the National Right to Life Committee, where pro-lifers from all over the country would meet to discuss political action, a few kindred spirits would hold their own workshops on more direct confrontational techniques. Activists from different regions would meet at the conventions occasionally (if they could afford the travel costs), swapping news and discussing tactics.

Eventually the most militant activists set up their own network. Scheidler had already established his Pro-Life Action League; in St. Louis, John Ryan set up the Pro-Life Direct Action League. The similarity in names underlined the group's common purpose. In 1984, the two groups called on their own network and rounded up activists from various other small organizations, drawing a total of 200 activists to a first national convention in Fort Lauderdale, Florida.

Joan Andrews learned firsthand about the lack of communications among pro-lifers. In 1978 she had come to the National Right to Life convention in St. Louis along with her sister, surprised and delighted to find a flyer advertising sit-ins at local abortion clinics. But she could not attend the event; her sister was engaged to be married, and her shower was scheduled for the same day. When they arrived back at the convention, the Andrews sisters could not find anyone to tell them about the sit-ins. By 1984, when National Right to Life convened in Kansas City, the advocates of direct action were much better organized. A substantial minority of the conventioneers expressed their willingness to take direct action against abortion clinics, and the local abortionists opted to close their doors until the convention was over. Buoyed by that precedent, activists took "the Kansas City pledge": from that day forward, whenever pro-life activists from around the country gathered in one city, they would take direct nonviolent action to save the lives of unborn children.

On the local level, the first powerful direct-action movement was based in St. Louis — ironically, the very city where Joan Andrews had failed to find it. The movement there was organized in 1979 by Vince Peterson, who passed the leadership on to Samuel Lee. (Lee, in his turn, would later step aside from the Rescue movement, turn his attention to legislative work, and help craft the Missouri law which eventually withstood a Supreme Court challenge in the historic *Webster* case.) By 1979, a half-dozen St. Louis activists had already been arrested for blocking an abortion clinic, convicted, and then acquitted after a successful appeal.

Led by Peterson and Lee, and manned by such pro-life stalwarts as John Ryan and Joseph Wall — who between them had logged several hundred arrests by 1990 — the St. Louis activists enjoyed an extraordinary burst of success. By early 1980, Samuel Lee could organize weekly protests at the local abortuaries. Whenever a woman approached the doors to procure an abortion, two pro-life activists would step forward — one for the baby, one for its mother — and offer themselves for arrest.

The cumulative impact of all those arrests was powerful. The local police dutifully arrested the pro-life activists, but they also contributed to their legal defense fund, and even hired a plane to fly above the site of the sit-ins, carrying a pro-life banner. In 1984 the St. Louis Board of Aldermen passed a resolution advising the activists "that they are not alone in their opposition to abortion on demand; they should worry not, but be of good cheer, for their essential position is true." Even the city's busiest abortionist, Bolivar Escobedo, was affected by the disruption. With his clinic losing several clients every week to the pro-life counselors, Escobedo asked to speak personally with one of the pro-life leaders, and then with a Catholic priest. Activists hoped and prayed that he would abandon his practice and return to his Catholic faith.

Then gradually the St. Louis movement collapsed. Newly installed as the city's Roman Catholic archbishop, John May stood in front of the abortion clinics and denounced the "illegal" protests. (At the time the archbishop spoke, no pro-lifer had been convicted of breaking the law.) Soon thereafter the abortion clinics obtained a court injunction against pro-life demonstrators. A few faithful activists such as Ryan, Wall, and Andrews continued to block the clinics, but they were promptly arrested and removed; no new recruits came to take their places. Once again the Rescue movement faltered. Dr. Escobedo expanded his practice, opening two new abortion clinics.

While the new direct-action movement flourished in St. Louis, pro-life activism was growing in the nation's capital as well. John Cavanaugh-O'Keefe, who would emerge as a prime mover among that region's pro-life activists, wrote of the early results:

"In 1978 and 1979, Mary Ann Kreitzer and Dave Gaetano worked to encourage the religious leaders of northern Virginia to lead a community response to abortion. The net result of their effort was a small march led by Bishop Thomas A. Welsh. The night before this march, an abortion clinic across the river in Maryland was torched (pro-lifers are still convinced that it was an inside job, especially since the abortionist's medical records were found in the trash a block away). Media coverage of the arson overshadowed the bishop's march and effectively deterred any action more forceful than marching."

The deterrent effect did not last forever. In May 1984, the Pro-Life Non-Violent Action Project organized the first massive blockade at an abortuary in Gaithersburg, Maryland, a distant suburb of Washington. About one hundred fifty people blocked the clinic doors, the abortionist was forced out of business for the day, and only a handful of pro-lifers were arrested. In November of the same year, forty-seven pro-life activists were arrested outside an abortion facility in nearby Wheaton, Maryland. Two days later, in a suspicious echo of 1979, that same abortion mill was bombed.

The seeds of activism had been sown in Washington, but pro-life activists still faced long odds. By 1980 the pro-life movement had helped dozens of politicians to earn seats in the U.S. Congress. Ronald Reagan, a late but welcome convert to the pro-life cause, was headed for the White House. The political climate seemed ripe for a pro-life victory. When activists like John Cavanaugh-O'Keefe warned that no political change was forthcoming, lobbying for direct action to save the unborn children instead, worldly-wise political activists (like the author of this book) dismissed him as hopelessly naïve. Alas, those "naïve" pessimists were right; the killing of unborn children continued unabated, regardless of the Reagan presidency.

Pope John Paul II had visited Washington in 1979 and issued a bold challenge to the quarter-million people who greeted him on the Capitol Mall: "When life before birth is attacked, we will stand up." In 1987 the Pontiff planned another trip to the United States, and an ad hoc group took up his challenge. Taking its name from the Pope's words — "We Will Stand Up" — this activist campaign planned to honor the Roman Pontiff by closing down the abortion business in each city that he visited. Over a hundred pro-life organizations (including Human Life International, Judie Brown's American Life League, and a host of small local groups affiliated with the Pro-Life Action Network) pledged their support for the "We Will Stand Up" campaign and its philosophy of scrupulous nonviolence. Since police officials would have their hands full with crowd-control duty during the papal tour, "We Will Stand Up" leaders urged abortionists to close shop voluntarily while Pope John Paul was in town. If the abortionists refused, organizers warned, they would face sit-in protests:

> ". . . if the truce fails and somebody decides to kill a child during the Pope's visit, we will assemble as many generous people as possible, to kneel in front of the abortion clinic, praying for peace in the family. We will not leave voluntarily until we are sure there will be no executions that day."

"We Will Stand Up" attracted very little notice from the organizers of the papal tour — who viewed the campaign with considerable misgivings — and still less attention from the secular journalists who flocked around the Pope's entourage. Nevertheless the effort scored a remarkable success. In Miami, where Pope John Paul began his American tour, all sixteen aborturaries were voluntarily closed. In the smaller cities on the tour (Columbia, South Carolina, and Monterey, California), abortionists again stopped business to avoid trouble. In New Orleans three abortion mills closed voluntarily, and another was closed by a pro-life barricade; twenty-one people were arrested. In Phoenix seven clinics closed, and again pro-lifers successfully blockaded one that remained open.

By the time the jets carrying the papal entourage reached the West Coast, the "We Will Stand Up" activists lagged far behind in the cars. The abortion industry was active in Los Angeles and San Francisco, although some pro-lifers staged blockades in each city. But when the Pope reached Detroit for the final stop of his American journey, the pro-life activists had regrouped. Most of that city's aborturaries quietly closed for the day. Again a huge pro-life contingent arrived at one busy clinic, and again one open clinic was temporarily paralyzed by a pro-life barricade. In its last and best organizing effort, "We Will Stand Up" had recruited two hundred people to block the doors in Detroit, establishing a new high-water mark for pro-life activism.

By now every American pro-life activist had heard about the Rescue movement. The sponsors of the "We Will Stand Up" campaign included the most experienced activists and the most creative publicists in the young movement, including Joe Scheidler and Joan Andrews, Juli Loesch and John Cavanaugh-O'Keefe. Among themselves, those sponsors noted in a recruiting pamphlet, "We have closed abortion clinics repeatedly. On five occasions we have closed down the whole abortion industry in an entire city." They had emerged from the fringes and begun to tweak the consciences of more conventional pro-life groups. But they remained miles outside the American mainstream. Politicians and media personalities could safely ignore them, and did. The few pro-life political lobbyists who had managed to command a bit of media attention — most notably the leaders of the National Right to Life Committee and the Roman Catholic bishops — took great pains to distance themselves from anyone who refused to "work within the system."

Oddly enough, although the growing movement had developed a consistent philosophy of nonviolence, and a warehouse of powerful arguments to justify their activism, one key ingredient was still lacking. The pro-life activists had no succinct phrase to describe exactly what they were doing on the sidewalks outside the aborturaries. Back in 1970 Brent Bozell had called his effort a "demonstration." As late as 1988 Richard Cowden-Guido, in his introduction to collection of Joan Andrews's letters, referred to "tactical sit-ins." The word that would eventually emerge to describe this movement — rescue — did not appear anywhere in the "We Will Stand Up" brochure. Then a young New York activist named Randall Terry had an inspiration that gave pro-life activism its rallying cry and crystallized the emerging nationwide movement into Operation Rescue.

He began by counseling pregnant women on the sidewalks outside the clinics, but he constantly sought more direct, aggressive approaches to stop the killing. He imbibed the new spirit of activism from leaders like Joe Scheidler, and in 1986 he organized his first blockade at a nearby clinic. It was while he was serving a jail term for that effort, in March 1986, that Terry first envisioned something much more ambitious than the sporadic campaigns mounted by a ragtag handful of dedicated activists.

Terry was sitting in a noisy jail cell, he recalls, with the cigarette smoke hanging thickly in the air around him, when a biblical passage struck him like an electric shock. The inspiration came from Judges 5:2: "That the warriors in Israel unbound their hair, that the people came forward with a will, bless Yahweh!" Why should pro-life activism be organized as a guerilla campaign? Why not awaken Christian communities all over America and join them together in a massive, all-out assault?

Months would pass before Terry saw the first real test of his ideas. After explaining his vision to fellow activists, pondering and praying over tactics, he planned to introduce Operation Rescue in the media mecca of New York with a series of big blockades in May 1988. To make that effort successful he would need hundreds of new pro-life activists, and to recruit those new activists he would need to (as he later wrote) "spark momentum and demonstrate that Rescue missions could work." So Terry organized a sort of "dress rehearsal" for the New York debut, a blockade in suburban Philadelphia in the autumn of 1987. On the Saturday after Thanksgiving, more than two hundred OR recruits blocked the doors to an abortuary in Cherry Hill, New Jersey. When local police arrived on the scene, they were nonplussed to find a crowd that was calm, prayerful, and obviously not a bit threatening; more than three hours passed before they finally began to make arrests.

Dozens of pro-lifers were arrested, but the abortuary never did open for business that day. Three women who came expecting to procure an abortion found their path blocked, talked with sidewalk counselors, and decided to keep their babies. And the Cherry Hill Rescue finally brought headlines for pro-life activism. The Christian Broadcasting Network prepared a feature report for its *700 Club* program, along with the weekly newspaper the *National Catholic Register* and the monthly magazine *Christianity Today*. Operation Rescue had arrived.

Riding on the wave of that success, OR burst on New York as scheduled in May 1988. Well over fifteen hundred people, including forty clergymen, were arrested in a series of blockades. New York is not like any other city in the world. Every major media outlet has an office (if not editorial headquarters) in Manhattan. When a storm hits New York City, the whole nation hears the story immediately. The Cherry Hill Rescue had earned headlines in the religious press; the New York Rescues earned headlines everywhere. In 1987 every pro-life American knew about the Rescue movement. In 1988 the circle was much wider; now every *literate* American knew.

Suddenly the Rescue movement caught fire, just as Terry had envisioned and predicted and hoped and prayed that it would. In June the Rescuers were back in the Philadelphia suburbs, setting a new record when 591 people were arrested on one occasion, at an abortuary in the suburb of Paoli. Buoyed by their success, OR activists began to schedule blockades all across the country, and since 1988 was an election year, the sidewalk barricades thrust abortion into the headlines.

Now Randall Terry demonstrated a new facet of his leadership: the ability to seize opportunities. The Democratic Party had scheduled its national convention for Atlanta. Terry surprised even many of his top lieutenants with a public pledge to close down the abortion industry in that city. On June 19, when OR staged its first blockade in Atlanta, virtually no one recognized the importance of the event. But the Rescuers kept coming, again and again and again, forcing Atlanta to take notice. When autumn began, and the Rescues continued unabated, Atlanta police officials announced plans to "get tough" with OR. Soon those arrested were facing heavier charges and complaining of police brutality; still the Rescues continued. When the four-month siege of Atlanta finally ended, 1,235 people had been arrested in 24 separate Rescues.

During that siege, hundreds of new recruits had joined the Rescue movement, and dozens of longtime activists had gained courage and experience. OR exploded across the country. New cadres of leaders, battle-tested in Atlanta, began recruiting activists in dozens of different cities. Blockades became a regular staple of Saturday media coverage, rather than a newsroom oddity. The year 1989 began with another spectacular Rescue in New York, with over a thousand people arrested with the *Today* show and *McNeil-Lehrer NewsHour* capturing the drama on videotape. Then OR moved to the West Coast, to observe Holy Week with another series of high-profile blockades in the country's other media capital, Los Angeles.

Soon the Rescue movement was spreading so fast, and hitting different cities so regularly, that no one could keep track of all the stories. Thousands of new recruits — most of them people who would never have dreamed of risking arrest, even one year earlier — joined the ranks. OR leaders began to supplement their regular Saturday blockades with special Rescues organized around a particular theme. Washington, D.C., saw two such "theme" Rescues. There was Rachel's Rescue, organized and conducted by women, many of whom had undergone the trauma of abortion themselves. There was the Veteran's Rescue, for which hundreds of ex-servicemen dug their own military uniforms out of mothballs and blocked the aborturaries, citing their old oath to defend American lives. In the New York area, Rescue tacticians launched "Operation Goliath," setting up blockades again and again at one busy abortuary in the suburb of Dobbs Ferry. When the OR headquarters in Binghamton called for "National Days of Rescue," dozens of cities responded, so that the next day's newspapers would cover the pro-life activities with a sort of box score, cataloging the number of arrests in different regions.

By August of 1990, that box score told a story of staggering proportions. Since its first New York debut in May 1988, OR had scheduled 683 Rescues at sites scattered all over the United States. More than 60,000 people had risked arrest by blocking abortion clinics. Roughly 41,000 had been jailed. (On that index, the statistics for OR were already roughly six times as high as those compiled during the entire civil-rights movement.) Most important of all, there were "confirmed saves" — 568 babies whose mothers had stopped outside the abortuary doors and ultimately decided against abortion.

Week after week the Rescues continued, new recruits participated, and aborturaries were closed. But finally OR lost its momentum, for two reasons. First the novelty wore off. As the Rescues became almost a matter of routine, the recruits who came seeking adventure lost interest. Michael McMonagle, an Annapolis graduate who had emerged as the key Rescue leader in the Philadelphia area, explained that 1990 was "a year of retrenchment for the Rescue movement." Thousands of participants had lacked the commitment necessary for a long-term movement, he believed. "They'd get in it, they'd get a high, they'd picket a few times and then they'd leave."

Even before that retrenchment took place, the abortion industry had begun organizing its own counterattack. As the number of arrests piled up during 1988 and 1989, and as their business losses (measurable in the number of babies saved) rolled up into the millions of dollars, the abortionists began lobbying intensively for heavier criminal sanctions against OR. Prosecutors began asking the courts for heavy penalties, and a few sympathetic judges complied, sending a chilling message to would-be Rescue participants. Abortionists and their political allies filed lawsuits and won injunctions, so that Rescuers faced not merely trespassing and disorderly-conduct complaints but also more serious contempt-of-court citations.

The numbers of Rescuers arrested kept rising, but so did the stakes in the legal battle. Hundreds of resolute new recruits had made a firm commitment to pro-life activism, but thousands of others felt constrained to steer clear of ever-increasing criminal penalties. Pro-life activists who had been willing to spend a weekend in jail for the cause were understandably intimidated by the threat of one-year sentences. The blockades continued, and the Rescue movement chalked up new victories every month, but it was the same people being arrested; the movement that had grown geometrically for so many months now hit a plateau. By late in 1990 the recruiting drive had stalled.

Undaunted, the Rescue movement continued to stage blockades. The same stalwart few were arrested time and again — just as a cadre of dedicated Rescuers had kept up the pressure in St. Louis years earlier. Their legal problems were mounting; they spent an ever-increasing proportion of their time in court, facing arraignments and hearings and motions and trials and appeals and sentencing on their accumulated criminal charges. If and when they were convicted, the sentences were steeper, keeping them off the sidewalks again for longer periods of time. Unless the Rescue movement could somehow break this trend, and attract a fresh generation of new recruits, the final outcome seemed inevitable:

Eventually everyone willing to face the long jail sentences would be in jail, and the Rescue cause would collapse.

Hundreds of doughty activists were ready to continue the crusade, regardless of the cost. But thousands more were hanging back. They wanted to help, and they knew that their participation would afford some protection for the hard-pressed veterans. If thousands of new recruits joined the Rescue crusade, regardless of whatever legal penalties were on the books, prosecutors could not possibly enforce them; the prison system simply could not accommodate them all. Still, those potential recruits needed some assurance: that they would not be alone; that others would share the burden and the legal jeopardy; that other new recruits would join them, making it impossible for prosecutors to slap the maximum penalty on all participants; that the Rescue movement would continue, not gradually wither and die. For several months OR could not furnish that assurance.

Until Wichita.

2

Bleeding Kansas

IN KANSAS, at the geographical center of the United States, a quiet agricultural economy masks a turbulent political history.

Here in America's heartland, the battle over slavery first exploded into violence, and "Bleeding Kansas" became a harbinger of the Civil War.

When Congress opened the territory to settlers in 1854, the Kansas-Nebraska Act stipulated that a majority vote would determine whether or not the new state would allow slavery. Zealots from both sides of that issue poured into Kansas, punctuating their arguments with lynchings and massacres. The furies unleashed in Kansas illustrated what the Civil War proved: that an issue such as slavery, which involves irreconcilable moral differences, could not be settled peacefully within the American constitutional tradition.

Over a century later, during the summer of 1991, Kansas again became the testing ground for a moral dispute which has resisted all efforts at compromise. Pro-life activists from all over the country converged on the normally quiet city of Wichita, and — finding an irascible federal judge as their foil — staged a six-week showdown that again exposed the limitations of the American legal system.

In June, the national leaders of Operation Rescue announced plans for a special week-long effort to close abortion clinics in Wichita during the middle of July. Why Wichita? Rescue leaders pointed to the strong pro-life movement in Kansas and to the state's historic role in the campaign to eliminate slavery. But above all, the invitations to Wichita dwelt on the presence of Dr. George Tiller, whose thriving abortion business specializes in "late-term" abortions, performed in the second and third trimesters of pregnancy. American public opinion is queasy about abortion in general, but the grisly process of late-term abortion is particularly unpopular. During the second trimester (the fourth through sixth month) of pregnancy, the abortionist must literally dismember the unborn child, then painstakingly reassemble the severed limbs to ensure that nothing has been left in the womb. Late-term abortions are often accomplished by saline injection, which literally scalds the unborn child to a painful death in the womb. In the third trimester, the usual procedure is to inject digoxin into the baby's heart, killing it, then induce labor the following day to expel the corpse.

At the late stages of pregnancy, a normally developed baby can survive outside the womb; some babies have even survived after a saline injection. And for the mother, late-term abortion poses more medical risks than childbirth. For those reasons, only a half-dozen American doctors perform third-trimester abortions. Yet for Tiller the practice is a specialty. Promotional literature distributed by his clinic states that the only "limit" for an abortion comes when the baby's head exceeds 2.5 inches in diameter; his fees range from $1,850 to $3,000, as compared with an average fee of about $700 for even a second-trimester abortion.

In a nationwide television appearance, Randall Terry charged that Tiller performs ten to twenty third-trimester abortions every week. To support that figure Terry produced a letter from Lura Tivis, who had once worked as a clerk in the busy Tiller abortuary. Peggy Jarman, a spokeswoman for the Tiller clinic, admitted that Tivis had once been a "disgruntled" employee, but dismissed her figures as hopelessly exaggerated. Citing concern for patients' privacy, she refused to provide any more precise statistics, but claimed the real number of late-term abortions would be close to ten or twenty per year. Rescue leaders — who saw visibly pregnant women entering the clinic day after day — dismissed that figure as ludicrous. However often he actually does late-term abortions, Dr. Tiller certainly caters to the late-term business.

Tiller advertises his services nationwide, and a map on his office wall is cluttered with pins, representing his customers, scattered across all fifty states as well as Mexico and Canada. He leases rooms in a nearby motel to accommodate women who come to his clinic from outside Kansas. To dispose of the human body parts he accumulates, Dr. Tiller even operates his own incinerator, duly licensed for the disposal of biological waste. Although two other abortion clinics operate within Wichita's city limits, and OR would stage blockades at each of them, the principal focus of the "Summer of Mercy" campaign always remained on "Killer Tiller" —

described in a recruiting pamphlet as "the nation's most notorious child-killer."

All through June, the informal networks of pro-life activists buzzed with the news about Wichita. Soon dozens of seasoned campaigners from all across the country were forming car pools, packing a few bags, and converging on the Wichita Plaza Hotel, where organizers had negotiated a special "convention" rate of thirty-five dollars a night. OR's national leadership shifted its headquarters from Binghamton to a temporary "command center" in the hotel lobby.

The first skirmish of the "Summer of Mercy" campaign was uneventful. On July 16, some five hundred Rescuers blocked the entrance to a local abortion clinic. But the clinic had no business scheduled for that day; local abortionists had postponed their appointments for the week, avoiding a head-on confrontation. The next day Rescuers sweltered through hundred-degree Kansas heat, but again there was no confrontation. (When Rescuers suspected that abortions were being performed temporarily in a Planned Parenthood office, the office staff quickly offered a tour to defuse the rumor.) The crowd outside the abortion clinic had grown to nearly 800, but still the police had made no arrests; Lieutenant Don Deckert offered the cautious compliment that the Rescuers were "a more easily manageable group than we had anticipated."

Then OR dropped a bombshell. Speaking at a rally on July 18, OR leader Keith Tucci announced that the "Summer of Mercy" would extend beyond the original one-week plan. Explaining, "I believe that God intends us to finish what we're doing here," he urged pro-lifers to "pitch tent" in Wichita. The result was a seemingly instantaneous explosion in the number of pro-life activists. By Friday night Randall Terry addressed a high-spirited crowd of over two thousand Rescuers. OR promised a twenty-four-hour daily vigil to ensure that the clinics would remain closed.

Quickly building momentum, OR churned out twenty-one thousand letters to pro-lifers all across the country, beckoning them to Kansas. The Wichita Plaza Hotel, which had never before seen a convention held over past its scheduled dates, happily cut the special rate to twenty-five dollars a night and allowed Rescuers to crowd three or four into one room. For the abortionists, a one-week disruption was an inconvenience; an indefinite blockade was disastrous. Peggy Jarman, who handled public relations for Dr. Tiller, assured reporters that the clinic would keep its appointments — many of which had already been postponed. Bracing for a showdown on Monday, twelve hundred people joined a rally in support of legal abortion. Speakers representing OR fanned out to speak at nineteen different churches on Sunday morning, generating an enthusiastic crowd of fifteen hundred for their own rally, and OR national director Patrick Mahoney predicted that six hundred pro-lifers would risk arrest the following day. For the first time, the confrontation hit the front page of the local daily newspaper, *The Wichita Eagle*.

The battle began on schedule that Monday morning. Scores of Rescuers blocked the entry to Tiller's clinic, braving a brutal Kansas heat wave that drove midday temperatures above 105 degrees. Police on horseback plowed through the blockade, clearing the way for the police vans that carried Dr. Tiller, his staff, and his customers into the building. Randall Terry complained bitterly about police tactics: the horses, which had been prancing dangerously close to seated Rescuers; the use of Mace, which police officials first denied, then later admitted; but above all the use of police vans as free public transportation for the abortionist. Wichita police arrested 14 Rescuers on Monday, a modest total after so much publicity. But that proved to be only a preliminary skirmish; the real battle erupted on the following day. The abortuary, still working off its backlog from the previous week's closing, had a full schedule of appointments. The Wichita police, having reconsidered their tactics, eschewed the horses, the Mace, and the shuttle vans. Again, several hundred Rescuers blocked the door.

After repeated warnings and fruitless negotiations, police began making arrests shortly after noon on Tuesday. By mid-afternoon, only a handful of Rescuers remained in front of the clinic's doors. Fearful that the abortuary would soon be open, the Rescuers redoubled their prayers, begging that somehow the clinic would remain closed. To their delight, a few drops of rain turned into a cloudburst, drenching everyone on the site and severely hampering the police effort. Arrests continued at a snail's pace through the late afternoon and into the evening. Some of the first Rescuers arrested, having been released on bail, rejoined the blockade. OR leaders, sensing a dramatic opportunity, hastily convened an evening prayer-rally on the street outside the clinic, and recruited new Rescuers to join the all-night vigil. By the time the last Rescuer was dragged away from the gates late Wednesday afternoon, the clinic had been closed for nearly thirty-six hours; altogether, police had made four hundred arrests.

From the moment that downpour began on Tuesday afternoon, OR leaders believed that the "Summer of Mercy" was something much more than just another civil-disobedience campaign. Participants unabashedly spoke of miracles, and claimed that the Holy Spirit had touched their movement. This summer in Wichita would form a watershed for the pro-life movement, they believed. Rev. Phil Vollman, an Evangelical pastor from Cleveland, told the Catholic News Service: "This is the first national event where we have had this kind of breakthrough — where the entire death industry shut down."

"This is the way it ought to work," Rev. Vollman continued; "When the Christians come out of their churches and act like the Gospel means something out here, killers like Tiller ought not to be in business." As Keith Tucci had predicted a week earlier, "This is going to be a testing ground for taking back to every state in the nation."

Beyond question, the spectacular success of the Wichita campaign revivified the Rescue movement. New recruits were pouring into Kansas, with media reporters in hot pursuit. The normally quiet Wichita Plaza was a hubbub of activity, with an OR press office churning out releases in the basement and a CBS-TV camera crew permanently ensconced on the seventh floor. Every weekday night for six weeks, OR held rallies in the hotel's Garden Room; in a room that accommodates eight hundred, there was rarely an empty seat. Weekend rallies in Wichita's public parks grew impressively: four thousand participants one week, eight thousand the next. Virtually every morning the Rescuers were back in action, blocking entry to one of the city's abortuaries.

As the arrest toll climbed past one thousand, national news coverage steadily increased. Even the gray *New York Times*, which had studiously underplayed the Rescue movement, finally broke down and placed the Wichita story on the front page for August 12 — when the Summer of Mercy was four weeks old, and the arrest total had already topped fifteen hundred.

Still more important, OR galvanized the pro-life community of Kansas. Passing the hat at every rally, OR brought in enough revenues to support an imposing campaign. The Newman Center at Wichita State University offered free dinners for Rescuers; dozens of free doughnuts were delivered to the hotel lobby every morning. When OR announced a special Rescue for members of the clergy, local pastors responded in droves; 83 priests and ministers were arrested in one day. Rev. Robert Hemberger, chancellor of Wichita's Catholic diocese, remarked: "There are a lot of people examining their consciences here." The arrest records confirmed that observation. At first the Summer of Mercy campaign had been dominated by out-of-state Rescuers. By August 14, nearly half of the Rescue arrests — 859 of a total of 1,773 — involved Wichita residents. Some sources of support were unexpected, and some unusually influential. Wichita Police Captain Mike Watson bowed his head to join the Rescuers in prayer before he began arresting them. Another police officer helpfully repeated the instructions which OR marshals were shouting to Rescuers: "Drop to your knees. Stop when I touch you." The Catholic bishop, Eugene Gerber, joined the crowd outside the abortuary on the day of the clergymen's Rescue, and although he did not join the blockade, he announced, "I am certainly in solidarity with them." And on August 2, OR scored an unprecedented coup when Kansas Governor Joan Finney addressed their rally, praising the pro-life activists for the "orderly manner and dignity with which you have conducted yourselves." While she urged the Rescuers to "please work within the law," the Governor also confirmed her reputation as a staunch pro-life advocate by remarking that "it is the character and the courage of our state which is at risk."

* * *

If that fateful rainstorm on July 23 was the first crucial event in the Summer of Mercy campaign, the second development — equally crucial — began to unfold on the same day, in a federal courthouse across town. Two of Wichita's abortion clinics had launched a federal lawsuit against OR, seeking an injunction to stop the clinic blockades. Their suit was based on an obscure nineteenth-century federal law, originally passed by Congress in the aftermath of the Civil War to halt Ku Klux Klan harassment of the black Americans newly freed from slavery. The abortionists argued that just as the Klan aimed to curtail the rights of black Americans, OR systematically attempted to oppress women by denying them access to abortion. (This odd use of the 1871 Ku Klux Klan act was not entirely unprecedented; in 1989 a Virginia federal court had cited the same statute in an injunction; that case, *Bray v. Alexandria Women's Health Clinic*, eventually reached the Supreme Court.) Federal Judge Patrick Kelly accepted that argument and issued a temporary restraining order barring any effort to block the clinics.

OR leaders were not deterred by Kelly's order; the Rescue movement had faced injunctions many times before. Randall Terry appealed to a higher authority, remarking, "We have our own injunction in the Bible." Patrick Mahoney added, "Judge Kelly's injunction has only emboldened the people." The Rescues continued without a pause the next day, and Judge Kelly, described by *The Wichita Eagle* as "visibly angry" by that defiance, ordered Terry and Mahoney jailed for contempt of court.

While Judge Kelly pressed the OR leaders to accept his authority, the Rescue effort continued unimpeded. Terry and Mahoney refused to promise that they would obey the injunction, and rank-and-file OR participants would not have been influenced by such a promise in any case. Terry told reporters, "Our own people would string me up if they thought that I'd made some kind of a deal."

So while Judge Kelly watched in mounting frustration, the blockades continued. By now the Wichita police had spent $250,000 in their efforts to keep the aborturaries open, and Mayor Bob Knight — who, like Governor Finney, makes no secret of his pro-life convictions — had instructed the police to avoid dangerous confrontations, allowing Rescuers to set up their blockades before making arrests. Police would do their best to clear a path into the aborturaries, but they would not arrest everyone outside. As City Manager Chris Cherches explained the policy, "We'll be there when the people are denied access. We are not going to be there as security guards." Unsatisfied with that policy, Judge Kelly met privately with Mayor Knight. Evidently the meeting produced no agreement, because three days later, when he heard reports that the Tiller clinic had been blocked again, the judge ordered federal marshals to clear the entrance immediately. Kelly bitterly complained that he had "called on the Mayor to make a public statement that they have no right to block entry." Now, he said, his patience with local government officials was exhausted: "I don't care what the city says at this point."

Mayor Knight shot back in an angry letter to Judge Kelly: "The city has been successful in controlling the situation, making arrests of persons who violate the law, opening access to the clinics and maintaining the peace, all without violence or injury." While the Wichita police were adequately enforcing the law, the Mayor argued, Judge Kelly was pursuing a more ambitious agenda. During their private meeting, he reported, Kelly had spoken about "breaking the back" of the national Rescue movement.

Within a week Kelly released Terry and Mahoney, announcing that they had agreed to respect the injunction. The OR leaders denied that they had done any such thing. Mahoney asked for a meeting with the judge to clear up the apparent misunderstanding; Kelly declined. Amidst that confusion, the judge scheduled an August 6 hearing to determine whether he should make his order permanent. In the face of a result he clearly saw as inevitable, Randall Terry expressed calm confidence in his cause. "I'm not calling you to civil disobedience," he told supporters at an OR rally on the eve of the hearing; "I'm calling you to biblical obedience."

Kelly did continue the injunction — and much more. He ordered OR leaders to pay a hundred-thousand-dollar "peace bond" in anticipation of future legal costs, and directed federal marshals to arrest anyone obstructing access to the aborturaries. In a fist-pounding display of judicial pique, he warned Rescuers that if they challenged his authority, "They should say farewell to their families and bring their toothbrush, and I mean it."

Still he was not finished. Outside the courtroom, Kelly told a press conference that he was disgusted with local officials — "I no longer listen to them" — as well as the "hypocrites" of OR. Lashing out in all directions, Judge Kelly invoked a chilling threat against activist churches: if clergymen supported Rescue activities, he warned, their parish properties might be subject to fines.

As a *New York Times* reporter summarized the outburst, Kelly threatened "to jail anyone who defied his order, including the Kansas governor, Joan Finney, and the bishop of Wichita's Roman Catholic diocese, Eugene Gerber."

"I have never seen in my life a judge this out of control," a stunned Randall Terry told reporters. "He mocked the mayor, he mocked the governor, he mocked the police department, he mocked the Christian community." If this was to be a battle of wills, Judge Kelly would soon learn that OR leaders could not be cowed easily. On the contrary, a hard-driving personality such as Terry's seemed to draw renewed energy from the showdown. And Patrick Mahoney, a hyperkinetic bundle of energy even under the calmest circumstances, positively blossomed in response to Kelly's pressure. For his appearance in federal court, Mahoney sported a toothbrush, prominently displayed in his shirt pocket. Later, when Kelly scoffed at OR leaders for issuing statements from the safety of their hotel, Mahoney immediately rose to the bait: "Tell Judge Kelly to bring out federal marshals tomorrow and arrest me, because I will be on-site tomorrow!"

As the Wichita case rose to national prominence, the strain on Judge Kelly became evident. "This has been the most awkward and stressful time of my life," he told *The New York Times*, adding that he had received a death threat. A lifelong Catholic, "The Judge also said he had stopped attending Mass at his parish church because so many of the parishioners there held strong anti-abortion views." An old friend told the *Times*, "Pat is a judge first and a Catholic second."

But if Judge Kelly showed anger at the August 6 hearing, he grew absolutely livid the following day, when OR appealed his order. In an unexpected development that again thrust Wichita onto the national news headlines, the U.S. Department of Justice entered a legal brief supporting that appeal.

The Justice Department's *amicus curiae* brief did not endorse OR. Rather, the federal government argued that Judge Kelly lacked the authority to intervene. The crimes with which Rescuers were charged — primarily loitering and trespassing — were not federal matters, the brief argued, and the Ku Klux Klan law did not apply to the case. As U.S. Attorney Lee Thompson explained, the Justice Department "takes no position on the activities of the litigants, but reiterates the government's view that the matters in litigation should be addressed in state court."

"I am disgusted with this move by the United States," Judge Kelly told Thompson. In a rare public violation of judicial neutrality, he appeared on the nationwide *Nightline* television show, explaining that he wanted "to speak to the Attorney General of the United States." Insisting that there would be "mayhem and distress" if his injunction was overturned, Kelly added that "there will be bloodshed in the streets of this city if I am forced to remove the marshals." Those warnings were disingenuous as well as hyperbolic. As a sitting federal judge, Kelly could easily "speak to the Attorney General" without requiring a nationwide television forum. And the federal government had no plans to "remove the marshals"; on the contrary, the Attorney General had specifically instructed federal marshals to continue enforcing Judge Kelly's order until the Tenth District Court ruled on the appeal. Clearly Judge Kelly pictured himself as an active party at war with OR, rather than a judicial arbiter handling a complicated issue. Indeed one Rescue activist, Rev. Joe Foreman, urged Kelly to excuse himself from the case, saying: "He's got to decide: does he want to be a talk-show host, or does he want to be a judge?"

By now the confrontation between Kelly and OR had become the main story in Wichita. "Why has this particular protest received so much attention while similar acts elsewhere have been little more than a local story?" William Bradford Reynolds asked in a *New York Times* essay several weeks later. The man who was Reagan Administration's top civil-rights official answered his own question: "U.S. District Judge Patrick Kelly in Wichita deserves the credit and the blame."

While Judge Kelly's crusade drew the nation's attention to Wichita, new actors took center stage on the weekend of August 24-25. Earlier in the month, the National Organization for Women had sent out fifteen thousand letters to abortion-rights supporters, urging them to meet in Wichita for a massive Saturday rally. A coalition of pro-life groups quickly countered, preparing ten thousand invitations to their own rally that Sunday. Unfortunately, the pro-life groups suffered a fatal breakdown in their communications; everyone thought that someone else was responsible for the final mailing. So it happened that several days later the Wichita Plaza staff found those ten thousand invitations sitting in an otherwise empty room. The letters had never been mailed!

When August 24 arrived, about 5,000 abortion advocates gathered on the banks of the Arkansas River. The rhetoric was brave: Eleanor Smeal of the Fund for a Feminist Majority announced that "Operation Rescue is a mere footnote, a pathetic, miserable little footnote in political history." But organizers could not conceal their disappointment with the size of the crowd. That disappointment was intensified when a coalition of rural groups, meeting in Wichita that same morning, spontaneously organized a motorcade of farm equipment; some three hundred tractors, festooned with pro-life banners, rumbled slowly, noisily past the downcast pro-abortion activists.

The response to the pro-life "Hope for the Heartland" rally, on the other hand, soared far beyond the organizers' dreams. Expecting good weather — and unaware of the snafu that had caused the invitations to go unmailed — pro-life activists had confidently predicted a crowd of ten thousand. They were wrong. At least thirty-five thousand buoyant pro-lifers packed the Wichita State University stadium to hear speeches by pro-life champions including televangelist Pat Robertson, author George Grant, and Catholic Bishop Eugene Gerber. During the rally, a rented airplane passed overhead carrying a banner that read: "Go home. Wichita is pro-choice." The noisy crowd in the stadium below boomed out its response: "We *are* home! We *are* home!"

Although he was the center of attention, Randall Terry did not appear at the Hope for the Heartland rally. In fact he was not even in Wichita. Earlier that week, a seething Judge Kelly had ordered Terry, Tucci, Mahoney, and three other OR leaders jailed indefinitely for failing to post the hundred-thousand-dollar bond he had assessed. This time the judge poured on the penalties: an immediate ten-thousand-dollar fine for each defendant, and another five-hundred-dollar fine daily for the next ten days, after which federal authorities would be authorized to seize their homes and garnishee their wages to pay their penalties. To avoid those penalties, Kelly demanded that the OR leaders pledge obedience to his order, in the presence of television cameras. Lawyer Pat Monaghan complained, "What the judge is saying is they would be allowed to get out if they make the right political statements. What you're trying to do then is literally bankrupt an individual for his political beliefs."

When Judge Kelly issued that extraordinary order on August 20, four of the leaders he named had already left Wichita. Two had returned permanently to OR's permanent headquarters in Binghamton, New York. Terry and Mahoney had traveled to Kennebunkport, Maine, in an unsuccessful effort to speak with President George Bush. (Bush declined to hear the Rescuers' complaints, with a dismissive comment that "everybody ought to obey the law" — although at the same time he was praising the civil-disobedience campaign that was radically reshaping the government of the Soviet Union.)

When Patrick Mahoney returned from Maine, he was promptly arrested at the Wichita airport by federal marshals. Keith Tucci was taken into custody by federal marshals at the local KSGL radio station, where he was just finishing an interview show. Terry, who was due back in Wichita later in the week, temporarily postponed his return.

Ironically, the national leaders of OR had planned to leave Wichita even before Judge Kelly ordered their arrest. By prior agreement with the hometown OR leaders in Wichita, the national headquarters had decided to leave town on August 25, turning the direction of the burgeoning movement back to the local group. The OR leaders were loath to back off their showdown with Judge Kelly — Michael McMonagle even commented the judge was "making it hard for us to leave town." But the local OR leaders were becoming impatient, chafing for the opportunity to resume control of their reinvigorated movement and insisting that the national leaders stick to their original agreement. Learning of those plans, Judge Kelly offered to free the national leaders if they would guarantee that the Summer of Mercy campaign was over.

After a few days of confused negotiations, Kelly announced victory. The OR leaders had accepted his demands, he reported, and they were therefore free to leave town. But as soon as they were released, Tucci and Mahoney told reporters that they had not given the judge any such guarantees, and indeed Kelly's order insisted only that they would leave town promptly — as they had already planned to do. (The Order of Release stipulated that "defendants were planning on leaving Wichita on August 26, 1991, prior to their incarceration, and upon release defendants will be permitted to leave Wichita.") OR, too, claimed victory in the showdown.

When Judge Kelly heard those comments by the OR leaders, his anger was rekindled. The next morning, in his most draconian order to date, he ordered the immediate arrest of any OR national leader who had not left Wichita by 2:30 that same afternoon. Now OR's leaders had had enough. They planned to leave town anyway; they had other battles to fight; they saw nothing to gain by prolonging their resistance against Kelly's judicial vendetta. When that final deadline arrived on August 30, a reporter from *The Wichita Eagle* caught one OR leader, Mike McMonagle, at the airport awaiting his flight. "What you're seeing is a scene reminiscent of the Old West," McMonagle observed; "We're being run out of town."

Suddenly Wichita was calm again. By Labor Day the Wichita Plaza Hotel, which had been packed to capacity for the Hope for the Heartland rally, was virtually deserted. The local affiliate of OR would remain in Wichita, to be sure, but local leader Michael Dodds confessed that with the national campaign finished, "To be honest, we don't have those kinds of numbers."

Still the drama had not quite ended. When the national OR leaders left town, fifty-nine less famous Rescuers remained in Wichita's jails, charged with violating Kelly's injunction. (Not all of those who remained imprisoned were pleased to see their leaders — now happily home with their families — complain to the press about violations of their constitutional liberties.) And on September 6 the *Phil Donahue Show*, which specializes in televised controversy, planned a live broadcast from Wichita's Century Center auditorium; Randall Terry was invited to appear.

On the day before that telecast, Judge Kelly called lawyers from both sides of the abortion issue into his chambers to discuss his final order imposing rules for conduct outside Wichita's abortuaries. The judge had meticulously crafted a plan detailing how many picketers could march outside the clinics, how much literature they could distribute, and a host of other niceties. Having vowed to "break the back" of Operation Rescue, he now detailed his own vision of how pro-life activists could work within the law. Like the OR leaders, Kelly saw Wichita as a test case; he too hoped to provide a model that others might emulate.

One element in Kelly's proposed solution, for instance, involved Rev. Dan Bonner of Wichita's First United Methodist Church, who had proposed himself as a "neutral" arbiter of the dispute. Rev. Bonner — whose opposition to abortion was muted at best — asked for access to Dr. Tiller's clinic, so that he could make a report to the Wichita community on what "really" happened there. Kelly accepted that suggestion, and added that upon their release from jail, Rescuers should be required to assist Rev. Bonner in his work.

Rescuers were appalled by that suggestion. By their standards, Rev. Bonner's work — seeking a compromise between Christian churches and abortionists — was an appalling betrayal of their faith. They would have rejected Kelly's solution if they had been given the chance. But they never had that chance, because Dr. Tiller's lawyers had the first opportunity to comment on Kelly's proposal. Dr. Tiller, they told him, certainly would not allow Rev. Bonner access to his facility.

To Kelly's astonishment, the abortionists' lawyers flatly rejected the judge's carefully crafted solution, sharply criticizing his tolerance for pro-life activism. For the first time, they were questioning Kelly's impartiality and his ethical standing. Even before OR's counsel had an opportunity to speak, Kelly's hot temper found a target on the pro-abortion side of the argument. With Randall Terry on hand as a fascinated spectator, the Judge berated the lawyers for Dr. Tiller and his fellow abortionists. Seizing the moment, OR attorney Jay Sekulow asked Kelly if he would free the remaining fifty-nine defendants, and the Judge immediately agreed. In an odd epilogue to their personal rivalry, Judge Kelly and Randall Terry saluted each other with a warm handshake. An executive for the Donahue show asked Judge Kelly why he had released the remaining Rescuers from jail. As reporters stood by, Kelly answered with highly unjudicial, earthy candor: "Because the other side pissed me off."

*   *   *

The Summer of Mercy campaign was over. But pro-life activism was not dead in Wichita. On Saturday, September 7, local OR activists blocked entry to Tiller's clinic; fifty-three people were arrested. The following Saturday they were on the sidewalks risking arrest yet again. The struggle would continue. Before it ended, the Summer of Mercy had kept national attention squarely focused on the quiet city of Wichita for over a month. More than twenty-seven hundred people had been arrested for acts of civil disobedience; thirty-one babies were confirmed as saved. OR had a new lease of life. Leaders in Binghamton talked of a new strategy, in which Rescuers from different states would converge on one city at a time, hoping to duplicate the astonishing success that began with that fateful rainstorm July 23. Already dozens of pro-life activists were heading to Fargo, North Dakota, where a new siege aimed to shut down that state's only abortion clinic.

Perhaps Judge Kelly, after his extraordinary role in the Wichita campaign, deserves the final word: "If what happened here puts in place any precedents in this country, so be it."

3

Saint, Prophet, Bishop, Cop

THE RESCUE triumph in Wichita — the hundreds of successful Rescue missions that spanned the United States, from Boston to Los Angeles and from Milwaukee to Houston — required a huge sidewalk army of pro-life activists. To develop that force, in turn, required a sea-change in the attitudes of thousands of law-abiding American citizens. Ordinary Christians — most of them conservative in their political outlook and deeply suspicious of protest movements — had to abandon their belief that American society is fundamentally healthy and reach the remarkable conclusion that our culture is so profoundly immoral that righteous people must be willing to face imprisonment. They had to wrestle with their fears, weigh their risks, shock their friends and neighbors. Before joining the Rescue ranks, they had to overcome their perception that pro-life activists were kooks and their fear that others would now see *them* as kooks.

Rescue leaders had plenty of strong arguments to bolster their recruiting campaigns, but abstract arguments are not enough to start a crusade. From a purely intellectual perspective, the reasons for participating in Rescues changed very little from 1979 to 1989. Yet in 1979 only a few dozen pro-life activists were blocking abortion mills, and by 1989 the Rescue ranks had swollen into the tens of thousands. What motivated that enormous growth?

Fiery preaching certainly played a role in Rescue recruiting. Once the movement grew large enough to schedule mass meetings, newcomers could be captivated by the enthusiasm of the prayer rallies and the exhortations of the speakers. But by far the most effective recruiting tool was the personal witness of the veteran Rescuers themselves. Skeptical pro-lifers first learned about the courageous individuals who were sacrificing their own freedom to save unborn babies, then began to admire their courage and commitment, and finally asked that crucial question: "Why can't I do the same thing?"

44

Before Wichita, then, and before New York and Cherry Hill and St. Louis, a few pro-life pioneers had to blaze the trail, plunging into the Rescue movement at a time when virtually no one supported them, and by their example win the admiration of more conventional activists. The first such pioneer to attract a national following was, fittingly enough, a young woman from the homeland of Daniel Boone.

Joan Andrews was born in 1948 in Nashville. Her father, trained as a lawyer, chose not to practice that profession, preferring life on a family farm in little Lewisburg, Tennessee. The Andrews household lived a somewhat unconventional life, largely impervious to the conventions of the outside world; everything revolved around the farm, the family, and the Catholic faith.

Joan herself was a quiet girl: very thoughtful, very religious, and painfully shy. In writing of her childhood, she emphasizes two experiences that made a lasting impression. In 1960, when she was twelve, her baby brother Joel was born severely premature and soon died. The entire family devised a burial service, right on the family farm. The tragedy was devastating, she recalls; "Still, I was very awed when I saw how perfectly formed Joel was. He was just beautiful. He was so little, and every little finger, every little toe, was so perfect." Young Joan was naïve about sex and reproduction, but especially after seeing her brother, she remembers with emphasis, "I knew babies were precious and knew they were from God, and I knew that a woman was pregnant *with a baby*."

That same fateful year, 1960, the Andrews family was picnicking beside a river when Joan's younger cousin slipped into a dangerous stream of rapids. Joan herself was a weak swimmer, and even as she plunged into the current she thought about two men who had recently drowned there. Somehow, with the help of her brothers, she pulled her cousin back to shore. But the truth is that she had *expected* to drown, and yet she could not see any alternative. Again her recollection is vivid, simple, and straightforward: "I could not choose to do nothing. Just watching was not an option."

The guilt of the "innocent" bystander became a recurrent theme in Joan Andrews' thoughts. As she grew older, she read extensively about the horrors of the Nazi Holocaust, and she wondered how so many German people could have stood by, passively allowing the butchery. Then those musings became horribly relevant in her own life: "In 1973 when *Roe v. Wade* was decided, I was shocked. I felt that we had returned to the world of Nazi Germany. I had always figured that we lived in a civilized world, but how that had changed."

Although her first solo mission to Chicago fizzled, Joan returned home to Tennessee convinced that she had found her life's work in the struggle against abortion. An educational misfit, she soon dropped out of college and moved to Delaware with her beloved sister Susan. She spent most of the late 1970s in Delaware, occasionally shuttling back to Tennessee, working for pro-life groups, picketing abortionists, and offering room and board to women facing crisis pregnancies. When Joan and Susan heard about blockades being organized by Vince Peterson and Samuel Lee in St. Louis, they avidly sought more information and tried to organize their own pro-life activist group in Delaware. When their recruiting efforts failed, they decided to move to St. Louis, to join the movement there, late in 1979.

Susan Andrews became engaged, and married David Brindle before the St. Louis movement organized its first blockade of 1980. But Joan Andrews was still there on March 8. In a mêlée at the entrance to an abortion clinic, a policeman accidentally caught Joan's finger in the door jamb and broke it. She left the scene, went to a nearby hospital for treatment, returned with her finger bandaged, and was arrested late that afternoon for blocking the clinic door again. The St. Louis group returned to block aborturies repeatedly throughout 1980, and Joan Andrews became a stalwart member of the Rescue team. From the early days, her devotion was extraordinary. Late in 1979, after being kicked by a horse on her Tennessee family farm, Joan had begun to experience dizzy spells and vision problems in her right eye. The blurred vision continued, but she was sure it stemmed from the accident, and postponed visiting a doctor for months. Finally, in April 1980, she had lost her vision in that eye, and she was forced to consult an ophthalmologist. He advised her to consult another specialist, but again she procrastinated, and it was May before she learned the grim news. The blindness was caused by a cancer behind her eye — a cancer that was certainly malignant, and quite possibly fatal. Doctors warned that the cancer could metastasize and kill her within a matter of months. Fortunately, the danger never materialized.

The doctors recommended immediate surgery, but Joan asked for a reprieve; she wanted to participate in a Rescue that weekend. The doctor relented, and the operation was set for the following week. On Wednesday, doctors removed Joan's eye. On Saturday morning that same week, she was back outside the abortion clinic, wearing a new eye-patch, risking arrest again.

By now anyone who knew Joan Andrews recognized that this was no ordinary woman — not even by the extraordinary standards of the Rescue movement. A few others (notably John Ryan from the same St. Louis group) risked arrest more often, and many others assumed more prominent roles in the leadership of the movement, but none could top the quiet intensity of this shy, thoughtful woman. Richard Cowden-Guido, who put together a book of her collected letters, captured her formidable dedication in his introduction: "The abortion culture cannot long endure the witness of a Joan Andrews. Either it will kill her, or she, by the grace of God, will destroy it."

Shuttling back and forth between Missouri and Delaware, she worked with Rescue groups from Philadelphia and Baltimore as well as St. Louis, then branched out still further to help Rescue organizations all up and down the East Coast. Living a transient, hand-to-mouth existence, traveling from town to town, constantly in and out of jail, she had dedicated her life entirely to the cause of protecting unborn children. When Pope John Paul II issued an encyclical letter (*Laborem Exercens*) emphasizing the value of human work, and insisting that every human person has the right to meaningful work, Joan read it with relish, taking it for granted that her own "work" was Rescuing. She even concluded that by holding her in prison, the American legal system was sinning twice: first by supporting the slaughter of unborn babies, then again by denying her the right to perform her work.

A legal system that could allow abortion, Joan concluded early in her career, must be thoroughly corrupt. The police who dragged Rescuers away from the clinic doors, the judges who sentenced them, the jail wardens who held them — all were essential partners in the system that upheld the abortion industry, regardless of their own personal views on the subject. She refused to play her own assigned part in that system; she would not cooperate.

In an autobiography, *I Will Never Forget You*, Joan Andrews summarizes her case for noncooperation:

> "To be free of any taint of cooperation in abortion you would have to stop paying taxes, grow your own food and set up your own trash system, just for starter. We are all implicated; the society we live in kills babies. And even if somebody did withdraw from American abortionism, there would still be the problem that it is wrong to tolerate slaughter in your neighborhood. There are no innocent bystanders at the execution of the helpless."

Joan Andrews could not personally overturn the legal system that supports the abortion industry, but she could reject its claim to moral authority. So she refused to pay court-imposed fines; that would be tantamount to an admission of wrongdoing. She refused to pay bail, since that money would help support the system. As time passed, her passive resistance escalated, and she refused to answer questions in court, or cooperate with normal prison routines. Of course, that personal campaign of noncooperation put her at the mercy of the legal system. But even in that weakness she found strength. Precisely because she was helpless, Joan found that she could identify more fully with the plight of the helpless unborn children for whom she was making all these sacrifices.

During her first lengthy prison term, a six-month sentence for violating a court injunction against Rescues in St. Louis, Joan's spiritual reading brought her in contact with an old Catholic theological tradition, the concept of "victim souls" — in her words, "people chosen by the Lord to pray for the world and to feel the pain that is always there when love renews something that is broken." She did not consider herself ready to serve as a "victim soul," but the idea helped buoy her spirits. She felt sure that the pain and isolation she experienced in prison could be transformed into a powerful spiritual resource for the pro-life movement. So even behind prison bars her Rescue work continued. She would identify with the unborn, offering up her suffering as a sacrifice on their behalf.

By the time she reached her fortieth birthday, Joan Andrews had been arrested over one hundred twenty times in Rescue-related activities and spent more than three years in jail. She could not block abortions from inside prison, but she could witness. Joan took an almost dismissive view of her jailhouse witness. "There is not a Christian I know who would not have been able to do a far more selfless ministry in prison," she wrote to a friend. But on that score she was profoundly wrong. Her letters from prison — packed with her prayerful thoughts, her unflagging concern for welfare of her fellow inmates, and her exhortations to the pro-life movement —provided invaluable inspiration for other activists. Rescuers began referring to her, only half-jokingly, as "Saint Joan."

Outside the Rescue movement, however, Joan remained unknown until her noncooperation policy finally provoked a vicious, patently unjust response. The crisis came in Pensacola, Florida. Late in 1984, three abortion clinics there had been bombed, and the resulting community outrage had withered the local pro-life movement. Joan volunteered to help rebuild the movement along nonviolent lines, and in March 1986 she brought John Ryan, Joe Scheidler, and others together there for a rally and Rescue. On that fateful day, Joan walked into the operating room at a local clinic, unplugged a suction machine used to perform abortions, and tried (unsuccessfully) to pull the electrical cord out of the machine.

Joan was arrested, of course, but that was nothing new. Soon after she was released on bail she headed back to St. Louis, joined another rescue there, and was arrested again. But while she was in jail in St. Louis, she learned that the judge back in Florida had revoked her bail. She hurried back to Pensacola, and returned to jail there on April 19, 1986. She would remain in prison — for the "crime" of unplugging an abortion machine — continuously until October 18, 1988.

Pensacola's abortionists had won a spectacular propaganda victory, skillfully blurring the distinction between peaceful pro-life workers and the handful of extremists who had carried out one isolated bombing rampage. In the public eye, the nonviolent Rescue of March 1986 was somehow linked with the clinic bombings of sixteen months earlier. Even erstwhile pro-lifers shunned the Rescue team. The public pressure on prosecutors and the hostility toward

Rescuers were unremitting. Joan and her fellow defendants faced veiled threats of "accidents" from their prison guards, while the city's Catholic bishop, Keith Symons, reprimanded the Rescuers for disrupting the peace of his community. After four months, Joan finally faced a no-jury trial. Judge William Anderson found her guilty on charges of burglary, malicious mischief, and resisting arrest.

Florida's sentencing guidelines recommend a sentence of twelve to thirty months for those crimes. But Judge Anderson sentenced her to five years in prison. On the same day, in the same courtroom, two men who had been convicted as accomplices to murder faced Judge Anderson for sentencing; they received four-year sentences.

From her conviction in July until sentencing in September, Joan was confined at Escambia County Jail. When she refused to cooperate with the prison regime, she was placed in solitary confinement. After her conviction she was moved to a maximum-security unit, the Broward Correction Institute in Miami. There too she ran afoul of prison officials with her practice of noncooperation and was consigned to a disciplinary unit. Although Broward houses the most hardened female criminals in the Florida penitential system, the normal stay for any prisoner in the disciplinary unit is less than three months. Joan Andrews remained in special disciplinary isolation for twenty months.

The rigors of isolation took their toll, but Joan was particularly hurt by the prison authorities' decision barring a Catholic priest from saying Mass for her. Outside prison she had attended Mass every day; for her, as for any devout Catholic, the Eucharist is the central act of worship, the font of spiritual strength. By denying her this opportunity to worship, it seemed clear, the prison officials were violating Joan's constitutional rights. But once again she received very little public support from Catholic Church authorities. After a sloppy, superficial investigation of her case, the director of Florida's Catholic Conference informed the state's bishops that Joan had been convicted of "injuring some people" — a charge which was completely unfounded — and placidly concluded: "It appears to me that the actions of the court and the prison system are appropriate."

Florida's prison system pulled no punches in the drive to break Joan Andrews. But she did not break. While her ordeal continued, faithful friends brought her story to the attention of sympathetic journalists. As word of her plight filtered out around the country, pro-lifers were appalled by what they heard. A ridiculously long sentence for minor crimes; month after month of punitive isolation; denial of religious rights: that sort of treatment might be the norm for political prisoners in a totalitarian state, but in America? The brutally unjust treatment of this one resilient woman forced hundreds of Americans to reexamine their ideas about the American legal system. If the stories were true — and further research proved that they were — then the cause of justice was truly endangered in America.

The months of punishment dragged on, but the pressure from pro-lifers began to mount. Thousands wrote and called Governor Robert Martinez, begging him to pardon Joan. Hundreds came to Florida, organizing rallies to draw attention to the mistreatment she was suffering. (One of the earliest rallies was led by a young man from upstate New York who was emerging as a key leader in the Rescue movement: Randall Terry.) Far off in Massachusetts, the State Senate passed a resolution commending Joan Andrews for her courage and adherence to principle. Still, despite all the pressure, the State of Florida remained unyielding.

Late in 1987 Florida authorities agreed to a complicated arrangement, in which Joan was transferred to a Delaware prison. There, in February 1987, she was able to participate in the celebration of Mass for the first time since her conviction. But the compromise broke down, and she was returned to Florida in June — to be greeted at Broward by a brutal strip-search that she considered almost equivalent to rape. She spent another long, slow year in prison there, alone with her thoughts and prayers, steadfastly refusing to cooperate with the system.

By now Florida officials wanted to be rid of this troublesome prisoner, but they did not want to back down. For her part, Joan's spirit was unbroken, and her pledge of noncooperation was absolute. At last, in early autumn of 1988, a friendly lawyer brokered a compromise. Joan was extradited to Pittsburgh, to face old charges for a Rescue there. As soon as the extradition was final, Governor Martinez signed an order of clemency, ending her sentence in Florida. The judge in Pittsburgh sentenced Joan to probation, and on October 18, 1988, she walked out of the Pittsburgh courtroom; for the first time in thirty months, she was free!

Ten days later, Joan Andrews was sitting on the sidewalk outside an abortion clinic in Toronto, ready to face jail again.

* * *

When Joan Andrews entered Escambia County Jail, the Rescue movement was a tiny, beleaguered group. The activists numbered just a few hundred hardy souls in close-knit groups scattered across the country, totally isolated from media attention. When they gathered for large-scale Rescues, they were delighted to find more than a hundred willing participants. By the time Joan emerged from prison, the movement had been transformed almost beyond recognition. Operation Rescue was now known across the nation, and scarcely a week passed without major media coverage of a Rescue in at least one American city. When the movement gathered in one place — as it had gathered in New York — thousands of people participated, and hundreds risked arrest. A ragtag band had become a powerful army.

What had happened? Three factors had combined to make the difference.

First, through her ordeal in prison, Joan herself had forced many pro-life Americans to recognize that their country was in the midst of a frightening cultural war, that it was time to take active part in the battle. Taking the fateful step into Rescue activities meant defying the law, and most pro-lifers are law-abiding, patriotic citizens, who hold a deep reverence for the American legal system. But now they realized that something was profoundly wrong. Not only were unborn children dying by the thousands every day, but when idealistic lobbyists sought to restrict the carnage, all their legislative efforts were stymied by the courts. The legal system was not working to save the innocent. Now, when one courageous woman sought to protect innocent children by stepping outside the law, suddenly the legal system worked overtime, protecting not the victims but the executioners! When they saw that same legal system bearing down with all its weight to crush this peaceful, prayerful woman, many Americans reached the unhappy conclusion that the system *deserved* their defiance.

If they had seen some practical gains in the conventional political campaigns, perhaps not so many pro-lifers would have taken the radical step into Operation Rescue activities. But conventional methods had produced no results; the rate of abortion climbed steadily, the death toll mounting by 1.5 million every year. Ronald Reagan, who unequivocally opposed legal abortion, was finishing his second term in the White House. President Reagan's public oratory on the subject had been invigorating, but the slaughter continued unabated. Even Governor Martinez, who for so long resisted all pleas to grant Joan clemency, had otherwise impeccable pro-life credentials. (When the Supreme Court's *Webster* decision lifted the ban on state regulation, Martinez immediately called the Florida legislature into a special session, in a valiant but fruitless effort to curb the abortion industry.) The pro-life movement had elected some of its own favorite politicians, but whenever pro-life lawmakers managed a meaningful legislative victory, they were frustrated by the courts — by the same judicial system that oppressed Joan Andrews.

Second, the Rescue movement had grown more sophisticated. Pro-life activists were building on their successes and learning from their failures. The movement's leaders were meeting regularly now, to compare notes, exchange tactical advice, and plot out new strategies. The public visibility of the Rescue movement was growing exponentially, so that anyone inclined to take a direct approach to saving children could readily find kindred spirits. Third, and perhaps most important, the movement had found a dynamic leader in Randall Terry, who gave the Rescue movement a new popular identity and organizational structure. His inspiration, which gave birth to Operation Rescue, found a resonant chord among America's most active Christians. His vision involved not merely a struggle to end abortion, but a campaign to restore the moral fiber of our society in general. Prayerful Christians, he preached in his powerful recruiting messages, must enter forcefully into the battle over American culture. His movement sought not just for social change but for moral revival; participation was not a political option but a religious imperative. If Joan Andrews was the "saint" of the Rescue movement, Randall Terry was its prophet.

"Child-killing is the flashpoint, the main battle front to which the divine trumpet is calling." Thus Terry calls Christians to action in his book *Accessory to Murder*. Abortion is only the most virulent symptom of a moral infection that has spread throughout our culture, bringing sexual promiscuity and homosexuality, divorce and adultery, pornography and alcoholism, AIDS and addictions of every description. Worse still, the moral decay has led Americans to *accept* those raging disorders, counting them commonplace, even inevitable. Randall Terry could not sit passively by awaiting the demise of America's Christian heritage. He heard — and sounded — the call to battle.

Born in upstate New York in 1959, Terry passed through a childhood distinguished only by signs of a restless spirit. As a teenager he set off alone on a trek across the country just before his high-school graduation, with no particular ambitions except perhaps to find himself. He found much more than he was seeking. When he returned home he was a committed Christian.

Graduating from Elim Bible Institute, Terry took on a variety of jobs to help support himself and his wife, Cindy. (Eventually there would be more mouths to feed — the Terry family's three foster children as well as their own.) He flipped hamburgers at McDonald's. He sold cars at Best Pontiac — affording his opponents the pleasure of referring to him, years later, as a "used-car salesman." (Even the conservative journal *National Review*, in a sympathetic article introducing the Rescue movement, used the same phrase to identify Terry.) But his true interests orbited around his faith, his church, and increasingly his desire to protect unborn life.

Terry's involvement on the front lines began modestly enough. In 1984 he and Cindy began pacing the sidewalks outside a local abortuary, trying desperately to dissuade women from entering, in an effort they called Project Life. At first their results were disheartening; they could not save a single life. But they persevered, and persuaded their entire parish to pray for their success, if not to join their picket line. Finally the dam burst. In one two-week period, five pregnant women turned their backs on the abortion chamber.

Once he had begun to persuade women to save their babies, Terry's next step was to open a Crisis Pregnancy Center, offering counseling, medical referrals, and material support for women facing crisis pregnancies. Soon that service was overworked, and he devoted countless hours of organizing and fund raising toward a residence for unwed mothers, the House of Life, which eventually opened its doors in 1987. Still Terry was convinced that he could do more. In 1986, after much prayerful reflection with his pastor, Terry organized his first blockade, and was arrested. It was while he served his jail term for that action that the full scope of Operation Rescue became clear in his mind, and he found his real vocation.

Others had similar visions for a pro-life crusade, but no other Rescue leader could match Terry's oratorical gifts. He pored over the Scriptures, especially the Old Testament, and preached memorable sermons about how the Hebrews suffered when they abandoned the Lord. He exhorted Christians to rid themselves of the passive piety that stops at the church doors. "The church for two full generations has been taking its brightest and best and saying to them, Be a pastor or be a missionary," he complained in a *Time* magazine interview. "It's time we took our brightest and best and said, Be a lawyer, be a judge, be a Governor, be the dean of a university, be the editor of a newspaper. We're involved in a cultural civil war. Right now there are very few Christians involved in the trench warfare."

Many mainstream Christian preachers shy away from military imagery. Not Terry. Asked to respond to a comment in the left-wing *Nation* magazine, which had described the abortion struggle as a "civil war," Terry leaped to agree: "Absolutely. It is a battle of ideologies, a battle for influence, a battle of allegiances, a battle for cultural dominance. There will only be one winner."

The stern message was worthy of a Puritan elder, but Terry did not look the part. Secular reporters might have expected to hear this sort message from a dour old misanthrope. They were puzzled to encounter a gregarious young man with a lively sense of humor, a flair for the media, and a thick mop of curly hair — every bit the child of his own generation. (One highly unflattering profile, published in the hard-left *Mother Jones* magazine, found it incongruous that Terry still used some of the slang expressions he had picked up in the 1960s; calling an unpleasant experience a "drag" and urging his friends to "dig it" when he made a telling point.) Terry's preaching style was always energetic. He spiced his presentations by periodically breaking into a dialogue between imaginary characters, or forcing his audience to respond by nudging — "Hello? Anybody home?" — after clinching an argument. Such lively presentations brought the media constantly to Terry's door, especially because the *Webster* decision thrust the abortion controversy onto the front pages just as Operation Rescue was hitting stride with its nationwide campaign of blockades. Terry recognized the power of the media (although he deeply resented their bias), and used their reports to further his message. He did not sugar-coat that message for popular consumption, nor did he temporize on controversial questions. When *Time* asked him whether he opposed the use of birth-control devices, he responded: "I believe that married couples who confess to be followers of the Lord Jesus Christ should leave the number of children they have in the hands of God." And when the *Phil Donahue* television show put him onstage opposite Faye Wattleton, the beautiful black woman who heads Planned Parenthood, he did not soften his argument that Planned Parenthood is a racist, eugenicist organization. On the contrary, in the circus-like atmosphere of Wichita's Century Center, he directed a personal challenge at his rival: "Faye Wattleton, I'm saying this to you: You have betrayed your race, You have been bought, Faye; you have been bought!"

Lively rhetoric like that drew reporters constantly to Terry, and he rarely disappointed them. Other pro-life leaders might promise to keep working for legislation to restrict abortion, but Terry would promise to close down the abortion industry in a specific city, at a specific time — the sort of concrete promise that makes for a hot news story. Other pro-life leaders could offer solid philosophical statements, but Terry would invariably say something more provocative about the decay of American Christianity, and provocative statements make for headlines. The reporters kept coming back; Terry kept OR in the headlines; through the unwitting instruments of the mass media, new recruits kept hearing and responding to the Rescue message.

Like Joan Andrews and other Rescue leaders, Terry began spending plenty of time in jail. He had been arrested thirty times before his thirtieth birthday. Before Wichita, Terry's campaign had culminated in the 1988 siege of Atlanta, an effort that eventually cost him a four-month sentence in a prison work camp. As the leader of a national movement which attracted thousands of voluntary donations each month, he also became the most popular target of abortionists' lawsuits. For his early efforts in New York, he was named as a principal defendant in a landmark suit, *NOW v. Terry*, in which the National Organization for Women charged that OR was engaged in a conspiracy against the rights of American women. NOW won the case, and the fines and damages forced Terry to close the offices of Operation Rescue, taking the operation "underground"; Operation Rescue-National soon emerged with a separate legal structure and bank accounts.

However, the costly investment was returning a dividend. New people were flocking to the Rescue movement from every direction, every economic and social class, every walk in life. Some of the new personalities in the movement brought their own publicity with them. Mark Bavaro, the All-Pro tight end for football's championship New York Giants, was arrested at a blockade; police asked for his autograph, and sportswriters clamored for an explanation. Dr. Joseph Stanton, a polio victim who had given twenty years of his life to the pro-life battle, hobbled to a Boston-area Rescue on his two aluminum canes, and spent a weekend in jail with Rescuers young enough to be his grandchildren; unable to sleep one night, he found a pencil and a spare roll of toilet paper, and scribbled out the moving "Letter From Brookline Jail."

Law-enforcement officials, caught between the rule of law and the demands of conscience, began to take their own stands. Long Island's pro-life district attorney, Dennis Dillon, flatly declined to prosecute Rescuers. Sheriff James T. Hickey of Corpus Christi, Texas, refused to order arrests at an OR blockade, because "I would be aiding in the murder of babies." The police chief of Redwood Falls, Montana, was fired by that town's officials after he missed six weeks of work; he was in jail in Fargo, North Dakota, with a dedicated corps of Rescuers.

Chet Gallagher, a Las Vegas police officer, made the most dramatic statement of all. Ordinary Americans might travel to Las Vegas on their vacation time, but in the summer of 1988 Gallagher went to Atlanta, where he joined Operation Rescue's siege. When OR came to Las Vegas, Gallagher tried to schedule a day off work so that he could join in the blockade, but he could not make the necessary arrangements. So when the day came he participated in the Rescue rally, led the caravan to the abortion mill, and left to report for duty. Then he returned to the clinic, acting in his role as police official. "I am sworn, trained, and committed to save the lives of innocent victims," Gallagher announced. He thereupon sat down on the sidewalk in full uniform, and was arrested alongside his Rescue colleagues. Gallagher, too, was soon stripped of his badge. He began traveling across the country, sparking recruiting drives for the Rescue campaign.

For Irish Catholic boys raised before World War II, policemen were symbols of unquestionable authority to be revered and obeyed. As a boy Austin Vaughan was no exception, and when he grew to become an auxiliary bishop of New York, his youthful impressions did not disappear. Bishop Vaughan is a pleasant, avuncular man, with a thick New York accent and a penchant for making jokes at his own expense. (He combines the two when he recalls one conference at which he spoke to a group of Evangelical Christian scholars. They were amazed by his presentation, he reports, not because they were unfamiliar with Catholic theology, but because they had never before heard it propounded by someone who sounded like Humphrey Bogart!) Bishop Vaughan was keenly committed to the pro-life cause, but he did not think of himself as a radical — and certainly not as someone who would defy the law.

The bishop's ideas slowly began to change during the 1988 presidential campaign. The primary elections in New York were hotly contested, and the bishop avidly read through the flurry of campaign statements, position papers, background analyses, and editorial endorsements. He looked in vain for any discussion of the abortion issue. Four thousand children were led to slaughter every day, and the issue was not even raised in the political forum! Bishop Vaughan was profoundly frustrated. Something must be done, he thought, to ensure that the issue is joined.

Then Bishop Vaughan was invited to speak at an event honoring Joan Andrews, who was still jailed in Florida at the time. He happily accepted the invitation, and was preparing remarks in which he would express his sincere admiration for the pro-life heroine, when the idea first struck him: If her act was justified, aren't other blockades justified as well? If she can do it, why not me? On the day of the testimonial dinner he met several representatives of Operation Rescue, who posed the question directly. Would he join? He promised to pray over the question.

As he was praying, the bishop's eyes were caught by the episcopal ring on his finger. The ring was a memento from the Second Vatican Council, given to bishops by Pope Paul VI at the close of Vatican II and passed on to Bishop Vaughan by an older bishop who had participated in the Council. Carved delicately into its face were images of Jesus, Peter, and Paul.

Jesus, Peter, and Paul. With a start, the bishop realized that all three had been imprisoned — and executed — by the unquestioned legal authority of the Roman regime. If a prison cell was good enough for the Lord, good enough for the first apostles, then it was good enough for Austin Vaughan.

The arrest of an active Catholic bishop, in the world's media capital, provoked another round of publicity. And Bishop Vaughan did nothing to quell the media furor when later, from his jail cell, he warned that New York's Governor Mario Cuomo was endangering his soul by his support for legalized abortion. But with his typical self-effacing attitude, the bishop dismissed his own importance. Nothing held him back from risking arrest, he pointed out; he had no family to support, no corporate duties to perform. As he concluded: "Nobody has less to lose than an auxiliary bishop."

His own humility notwithstanding, the powerful witness of Bishop Vaughan's actions — coupled with the calm, dispassionate arguments he delivered to audiences at Rescue rallies — brought many more new recruits into the Rescue campaign. Asked to comment on his auxiliary's actions, New York's Cardinal John O'Connor offered his complete support, sending reporters back to their editors by adding wistfully, "I wish I could go on a rescue." Was OR about to score its greatest recruiting coup in New York? Cardinal O'Connor fueled that speculation in a column written for his diocesan newspaper: "If [Bishop Vaughan] has to miss a Sunday Mass or a Confirmation because he is in jail, I'll be proud to fill in. Who knows? One day he may have to do the same for me for the same reason."

4

This Is Not a Demonstration!

HUNDREDS OF blockades have occurred, thousands of newspaper stories have been written, and still only a tiny fraction of the American public has even begun to understand Operation Rescue. Through years of experience in covering protest movements, journalists have acquired certain fixed reporting habits. Whether the protests are directed against military recruiters, nuclear power plants, or cuts in government welfare programs, reporters apply a formula to their coverage. Their stories will invariably list the number of demonstrators, describe their actions, and explain the political point they sought to dramatize.

When applied to OR, however, that formula provides inaccurate results. When they block entry to an abortion mill, pro-life activists are *not* trying to make a political point; they are *not* asking for government action; they are *not* seeking publicity for their cause. A successful Rescue might bring about all those effects, but they are secondary to the real Rescue mission. The goal of a Rescue is to stop abortions — not by influencing legislation, or swaying the courts, but by preventing the *particular* killings that were scheduled on that *specific* day at that *specific* facility.

When media reports speak of "anti-abortion demonstrations," therefore, they miss the point entirely. OR does not hope to "demonstrate" anything. A Rescue is not a demonstration.

The tactics of a Rescue operation are determined by the ultimate goal. In ordinary political demonstrations, protestors might picket or rally to gain attention for their cause. Once they have done that, they go home. Or to underscore their point and guarantee headline coverage, they might take concrete action that results in their arrest — climbing over fences onto a controversial construction site, perhaps, or pouring animals' blood over Selective Service records. In those high-profile cases, the demonstrators are giving a dramatic form to their beliefs, but the primary objective still is the same: to generate public attention and consideration for their point of view.

After they are arrested, the demonstrators can happily pay bail, hold a press conference, and go home.

Rescuers take to the sidewalks with a different objective. Yes, they want to dramatize the horror of abortion, and they might even choose targets with an eye to their public visibility. But their primary goal is to stop abortions. It would not be enough — in fact it would be completely self-defeating — to gather outside an abortion clinic, chant slogans, and then disperse when the police arrived. The abortion business would still continue, and the babies would still die. To stop the slaughter, Rescuers blockade the entries, physically intervening between the unborn babies and their executioners.

If and when police arrive to break the blockade, Rescuers do their best to continue the blockade without using or inciting violence. If they are thrown away from the abortuary doors, they pick themselves up and rush back, striving to regain their blocking position. If they are arrested, they drop into a limp posture, forcing the police to carry them bodily away from the scene. Even then, when they are handcuffed, they might crawl back toward the scene if they are left unattended. On rare occasions, when police agree to let them walk to the arresting vehicles on their own power, Rescuers will take "baby steps" — walking with a tiny, painfully slow, two-inch stride to prolong the process. Some ambitious Rescuers bring along bicycle locks, and lock themselves to each other or to the doors. These "lockdown" or "Kryptonite" (a popular brand of bike locks) tactics make the process of removing Rescuers especially slow, because the locks cannot be picked with skeleton keys, and only special equipment can removed the bolt without literally breaking the Rescuer's neck. As soon as the police finish their work, and the abortuary doors open, the killing can begin. So Rescuers use every available means to delay the clinic's opening, to buy even a few more minutes of life for the unborn children.

While the Rescuers bar the doors, a few other designated members of the Rescue movement act as "sidewalk counselors." These counselors, who are usually women, intervene with woman who are approaching the clinic. They offer literature on fetal development, tell them about the resources available to help with crisis pregnancies, and plead with them to spare their babies' lives. This sort of counseling can take place with or without a blockade, of course, and many devoted pro-lifers spend several hours every week pacing the sidewalks outside local abortion clinic. But if the blockade is successful in clogging up the entry, naturally the sidewalk counselors have more time to strike up a conversation with the pregnant women and make their arguments calmly.

Abortion-clinic workers deeply resent sidewalk counselors, and "clinic escorts" do their best to hustle women through the doors before they have a chance to hear the pro-life pleas. In fact some of the first "Rescue" efforts came when sidewalk counselors worked in tandem, with one approaching the women on the sidewalk while they other blocked the door, giving her partner a few more precious moments to use her persuasive powers. Some pregnant women listen carefully to what the sidewalk counselors tell them, others brush quickly past them, and a determined few respond with a burst of invective. But any experienced sidewalk counselor knows that her angriest foes will be the clinic escorts, who shoulder her brusquely aside, and the young men who bring their girlfriends to the abortionist. These men — presumably the fathers of the unborn children — are almost invariably very hostile, sometimes violent in their determination to make sure that the abortion takes place. Ideally, sidewalk counselors will have escorts of their own — preferably large young men — to deter any ugly outbursts.

If a Rescue bears fruit, sidewalk counselors reap the harvest. Even if the blockade is ultimately broken, many women will turn away from the clinic when they see a hubbub of activity at the door. Some of them, unfortunately, will reschedule their abortions for a different day. Others may decide against abortion, but the Rescue movement might never hear of those successes. Still a precious few women will stop, speak at length with the sidewalk counselors, and leave the scene determined to continue their pregnancies and bear their children. If a woman promises to reconsider her plans for abortion, the sidewalk counselors report a "possible save." If she agrees to accept help and decides firmly to continue her pregnancy, then the counselors can announce the most welcome news available at any rescue: a "confirmed save."

Between the sidewalk counselors at the curbside and the Rescuers at the clinic door, OR sets up a line of people whose sole function is to pray for the success of the Rescue operation. These "prayer supporters" do not defy the law or risk arrest, but they remain an integral part of the Rescue team. Whether or not the blockade succeeds, they will remain on the scene, singing hymns and praying for God's intervention to stop abortion, until the facility closes for the day.

Operation Rescue operates within a tight framework of self-discipline. Every member of the OR team — including prayer supporters, sidewalk counselors, and the rescuers risking arrest — is asked to take a strict pledge of commitment to nonviolence "in word and in deed." OR leaders appoint marshals to control their crowd and public spokesmen to address the press. All other participants are expected to focus their attention exclusively on their assigned tasks. Except for hymns, prayers, and instructions from the leaders, OR strives to maintain a prayerful silence on the scene. Even within the pro-life movement, some critics of OR question whether the movement takes a strong stand against violence. The answer is quite straightforward: it does. To become a part of the movement, before joining in any Rescue operation, a new recruit must sign a pledge. The exact wording varies slightly from city to city, but the pledge signed by the thousands of participants in the Wichita "Summer of Mercy" campaign is typical:

> I understand the critical importance of the Mission being unified, peaceful, and free of any actions or words that would appear violent or hateful to any witnesses of the event.
>
> I realize that some pro-abortion elements in the media would love to discredit this event and focus on a side issue in order to avoid the central issue at hand — murdered children and exploited women.
>
> Hence, I understand that for the children's sake, this gathering must be orderly and above reproach. Therefore:
>
> • As an invited guest, I will cooperate with the spirit and goals of the Mission as explained in [the OR campaign's recruiting brochure].
>
> • I commit to be peaceful, prayerful, and non-violent in both word and deed.
>
> • Should I be arrested, I will not struggle with police in any

way (whether deed or word), but remain polite and passively limp, remembering that mercy triumphs over judgment.

    ● I will listen and follow the instructions of the Mission's leadership and crowd-control marshals.

    ● I understand that certain individuals will be appointed to speak to the media, the police and the women seeking abortion. I will not take it upon myself to yell out to anyone, but will continue singing and praying with the main group, as directed.

    I sign this pledge, having seriously considered what I do, with the determination and will to persevere by the grace of God in Christ Jesus.

OR is a Christian movement, dedicated to spiritual struggle. Anyone who joins the movement will soon find himself caught in an emotional maelstrom. Pro-abortion demonstrators will scream and jostle on the sidewalks outside the clinic. Police will threaten and curse and perhaps deliberately injure Rescuers. There may be arrests, lawsuits, fines, injunctions, long prison terms. There is always the prospect of bodily injury. The media will misrepresent the Rescuers; "respectable" civil leaders will condemn them; friends and neighbors will question their sanity. Worst of all, when the blockade is broken and the abortuary doors are opened, OR participants will experience the emotional devastation of watching troubled young women enter, knowing that their unborn children are doomed, while the triumphant war-whoops of the pro-abortion demonstrators echo in their ears. This is a serious battle, not a Saturday-morning diversion.

Even while he exhorts Christians to join the front lines of pro-life activism, in his book *Operation Rescue* Randall Terry warns that some people should steer clear of the battle. "Are you a praying person? If not, stop!" he warns. "Satan will not give up this stronghold without a fight to the very end. Anyone who enters this conflict must be prepared for the spiritual battle of his or her life."

During the epochal struggle in Wichita, Catholic Bishop Eugene Gerber vividly sensed the spiritual forces engaged in the battle, as he explained to the Hope for the Heartland rally:

    "The first time I arrived near the site of a local abortuary I had a feeling that I have never had before. It is the feeling that comes from being in a place that is at one and the same time the most sacred and the most horrible. The sacred is the innocent unborn children; the horrible is the killing of them one by one. Only now am I beginning to associate the feeling. I imagine it to be the same as standing at Calvary where the most sacred and the most horrible came together."

For thousands of unborn children every day, the abortion clinic is their own personal Calvary. (Thousands of exploited women, too, will feel the trauma of abortion in their own lives, although the pain might not hit them until months or even years after the fact.) These babies are dying *right now*, not in some abstract formulation, but in a harsh, bloody, painful reality. For them the injustice of abortion is not a theoretical question, but a personal agony. Americans know (or can easily learn) when and where the babies will die, OR leaders point out. Why not take action to save them?

If abortion is the deliberation destruction of human life, if four thousand humans are surgically butchered every day, then the abortion industry's death toll surpasses any of history's most savage persecutions. Even the Nazi death camps claimed only twelve million victims, roughly *half* the total killed to date in our own nation's continuing Holocaust. Yet today we honor the courageous Christians who resisted Hitler's regime, and wonder why so many other Christians remained passive in the face of the horror. The noted Protestant theologian Martin Niemöller was one who resisted. When a friend asked him why he was in prison, Niemöller replied with a challenge: "And brother, why are you not in prison?"

(American history has its own version of Niemöller's pointed remark; Henry David Thoreau gave essentially the same answer to Ralph Waldo Emerson. In his essay *On the Duty of Civil Disobedience*, Thoreau wrote: "Under a government which imprisons any unjustly, the true place for a just man is also in prison.")

OR applies the same moral logic to contemporary America. "Christians have a tendency to fantasize about helping Corrie ten Boom or the Underground Railroad," Randall Terry cautions in *Accessory to Murder*. "What makes us think we would have aided them, when it might have cost us years in prison or even death?

Today you can save a life, and all it costs is maybe your reputation, a small fine, or a few hours or days in jail."

When OR leaders echo the challenge of Niemöller and Thoreau, they hasten to add that no American should be self-satisfied about his role in fighting abortion. For eighteen years since *Roe v. Wade* the casualties have piled up, and the Christian community has not made the sacrifices necessary to stop the bloodshed. No one — no pro-life activist, no OR leader — has the right to blame others for the American Holocaust. We *all* share the blame: for our failure to take action, for our passivity, for our lack of faith in invoking God's help to end the killing. Abortion could not have become an accepted part of our culture, OR argues, if the American Christian community had been on its guard. We failed — we *all* failed — and if we act now we should act in a spirit of repentance.

Intentionally or not, by taking that approach OR has satisfied the test of another great Protestant theologian, the American Reinhold Neibuhr, who instructed his students on the crucial difference between preaching righteousness and self-righteousness. A century ago, the abolitionist William Lloyd Garrison condemned all slaveholders as sinners. By that sweeping denunciation, Neibuhr argues, Garrison succeeded only in uniting the Southern slaveholders against self-righteous Northern preachers. If a preacher urges his congregation on a moral crusade, he must carefully avoid any air of moral superiority. Any such airs will invite resentment, and the point of the crusade is to stimulate resentment against injustice, not against the crusaders themselves.

Since we all share the blood-guilt of abortion, OR cautions Rescuers on the sidewalk to avoid thinking of the police, or the clinic escorts, or the women entering to abort their babies, as the enemy. The enemy is the moral evil of abortion, which has crept into so many souls because Christians failed to check its spread. Even the abortionists themselves are not the enemy. They may be sinners, but so are we all. If we have received the grace to recognize the evil of abortion, then we have an obligation to guide others toward by that same moral light. When Joan Andrews spoke to a group of former abortionists, she told them, "You don't owe us an apology. We owe you one because we didn't try to convert you sooner."

Constantly chastened by that call to humility, OR adapts its tactics to serve its moral goals. The need for a spirit of repentance is a constant theme of preachers at OR rallies, and acts of repentance are staples in the OR spiritual regimen. Even on the sidewalk OR manifests its commitment to humility. During the siege of Atlanta, when police blocked Rescuers from reaching the doors of an abortion clinic, OR looked for a way to press forward. If they marched up and confronted the police, the Rescuers might appear violent; they could risk losing their moral advantage, not to mention serious legal charges for assaulting an officer. So a dozen policemen, patrolling a street on foot, could hold off a battalion of nonviolent Rescuers. Just by posting a few guards, the abortion clinics could stop OR in its tracks.

Then Joseph Foreman, a prominent OR leader, made a happy discovery. If they crawled toward the abortuary on their hands and knees, the Rescuers could not be considered aggressive; there is absolutely nothing aggressive about someone in that posture. Moreover, if the police officers are standing upright, they must bend over into an awkward position in order to stop someone crawling toward them. When a police officer leaned down to put his hands on one Rescuer, another would quickly scuttle forward beside him. When the police touched any individual Rescuer, he would immediately fall to the ground, limp — but a colleague beside him would surge forward to the door. "The Atlanta Crawl" quickly spread to Rescuers across the country, proving enormously popular and effective. And Joseph Foreman cherished the posture for another reason: "It's about time we Christians were on our knees!"

Watching the growing sophistication of the Rescue movement, the abortion industry saw a need to hone its own techniques. From the earliest days of OR, abortionists insisted that their business would not be affected. No matter how thoroughly OR blocked access to an abortuary, the clinic officials would insist that abortions had proceeded on schedule.

In June 1988, the National Abortion Federation issued guidelines to clinics on how to cope with Rescues in the Philadelphia area. Since the public-relations impact was uppermost in the abortionists' minds, Alice Kirkman, the group's director of public relations, suggested that the clinics rehearse a few key phrases to use in press interviews. To squelch the impression that pro-life forces were rallying greater support, she recommended that the clinics announce that their forces were rallying by telling the press, "Actually, the experience has brought us more support." Remember, she made these suggestions *before* the blockades. The press duly reported those comments, however, treating the clinics' prepackaged, face-saving press statements as if they were citing objective facts.

Kirkman also advised the clinic operators to be sure that at least one employee was on the premises — even if it meant sleeping overnight in the building to be there before the blockade began. The purpose, of course, was simply to influence the press: "Even if there are no patient procedures on a demonstration day, the presence and continued work of their staffers can show that a clinic is 'open.' "

Once the blockade is in place, militant feminists can be counted upon to organize a counter-demonstration, aiming to discredit and demoralize the pro-lifers. In 1990 the National Organization for Women published a manual for such demonstrations, entitled "Project Stand Up for Women NOW." The manual advocated heckling the Rescuers, and mocking their hymns by singing parodies; the suggested titles included "Amazing Choice," "Jesus Loves Reproductive Freedom," and for the holiday season, "We Wish You a Safe Abortion."

Mary Meehan, writing on the abortion struggle for the *National Catholic Register*, unearthed an even more extreme pro-abortion effort in San Francisco. The Bay Area Coalition Against Operation Rescue (BAOCOR) advocated physically confronting the Rescuers even before the police removed them: "We are prepared to pick 'em up and move 'em out." BAOCOR pointed out that men involved in OR "have an inordinate sense of modesty and 'honor' about being accused of touching women. There are innumerable instances of clinic defenders neutralizing male ORs by shouting 'Get your hands off me; don't you dare touch me,' all the while they are tugging or pushing OR out of the line." Finally, BAOCOR recommended "sexual or religious baiting," blasphemous songs, and outright violence against the Rescuers.

When they employ such aggressive tactics, of course, the pro-abortion militants risk turning the police against them. And even the more subtle approach dictated by NOW has its strategic drawbacks. If hundreds of feminists gather on the streets outside the clinics, as NOW encourages them to do, many pregnant women see the commotion and turn away without waiting to learn exactly what is happening. So the abortion clinic loses business. In November 1991, NOW organized a massive demonstration of support for abortion in the Boston area, in response to reports that OR would stage a blockade there. The Rescuers foiled that effort by moving their blockade to a clinic in nearby Rhode Island instead. But the hundreds of feminists who had congregated in the Boston area stood their vigil, arms locked together in front of the abortuary doors, until they were sure the "danger" had passed. They did, indeed, prevent any pro-life activists from reaching the clinic doors. But they also prevented any abortionists, or any pregnant women, from entering the building! The clinics were effectively closed for the day — not by OR but by NOW!

OR tactics pose a puzzling challenge to pro-abortion activists. If Rescuers are arrested, they win some sympathy for their cause. So the strategy suggested in the 1990 NOW manual is "to avoid mass arrest of OR participants whenever possible." But if police do not make arrests, the blockade will remain intact. Since some Rescuers welcome the prospect of a jail sentence — as an opportunity to offer up suffering as a spiritual sacrifice on behalf of the unborn children — a few militant pro-abortion strategists suggest that the best way to penalize these people is by *refusing* to jail them. But if they are not jailed, they will soon be back at the clinic doors!

The battle of wits has produced a trove of wisdom within the Rescue movement. Rescue newsletters and OR veterans can offer advice on a host of arcane subjects. Lawyers connected with the movement can help Rescuers avoid damaging lawsuits, becoming "judgment-proof" by yielding control of their financial resources. Veterans of the movement advise newcomers on how to dress for a Rescue. (In cold weather, dress in warm layers. Do not wear restrictive garments. For modesty's sake, women might want to wear a body stocking or one-piece bathing suit, in case their outer clothes are pulled apart when they are dragged.) Rescuers learn that they cannot drink fluids before a rescue; the next chance at a restroom might be hours away. They learn to store personal items on their bodies for use in jail; toothbrushes and miniaturized Bibles are in special demand. Rescuers who have served longer jail terms can provide counsel on how to make prison life bearable. And a computer software package, Res-Q-Ware, has been written especially to help busy Rescuers keep track of their court appearances!

The steady progress of these new developments and the constant tactical cat-and-mouse game between Rescuers and police, or Rescuers and abortionists, lend their own excitement to Operation Rescue activities. No Rescue leader could deny the exhilaration that comes from thwarting efforts to infiltrate the movement, keeping the site of the Rescue secret, guessing the strategy of the police force, finding a ruse that will convince abortionists to open their doors, and finally arranging all the logistics of a blockade that will shut down an abortion mill for the day.

Still, the final measure of a Rescue's success is not the brilliance of the leaders' tactics, or the bewilderment of the opposition, or the emotional impact on spectators, or the number of people arrested. The one all-important index is the number of "saves."

Every save is a triumph; every save is dramatic. ("Unto us a child is born!") Every save is a miracle — the miracle of life — and sometimes the guiding hand of divine inspiration leaves clear fingerprints. In an East Coast city, a woman of American Indian extraction is literally lying on the table, ready to face the abortionist's knife, when she hears Rescuers singing hymns on the street below. Something touches her heart. She leaps off the table, rushes out the door, and asks for help bringing her baby to term.

Months later the same woman is sedated in preparation for a Caesarean delivery. A friendly attendant asks what she will name the baby, but her reply is unclear; her mind is already clouded by the anesthetic. Groggily she repeats a single half-remembered sound from her own Indian language: "Rasheem . . . Rasheem." In minutes a beautiful baby boy comes out into the world, and in their understandable confusion doctors announce the birth of "Rasheem". Only later do they learn the Indian meaning of that name: Rasheem, "the rescued one."

No, a Rescue is not a demonstration. When a weary novice Rescuer comes home from his first day in jail, and at the dinner table his own wide-eyed children ask for an explanation of why Papa was arrested (and why he missed their soccer games), he does not talk about the need for new legislation or the importance of making a bold social comment. He has an explanation that even a four-year-old child can readily comprehend.

"I was trying to save babies."

Still my daughter is troubled, and the next question flows naturally: "Did you save any?"

Thank God I can give the right answer: "Yes; three."

In a flash the furrows disappear from her forehead, and she attacks a hot dog with gusto. Breaking the household rule about talking with one's mouth full, she turns back to me with a triumphant smile. "That's great!"

5

Breaking the Law

WHAT SHOULD we say to our children — and to their children after them? That question furnishes the bottom-line challenge for Randall Terry's recruiting pleas. He asks the members of his audience to imagine that years have passed and their grandchildren are asking questions about the "old days" when Americans were killing unborn children. You can be sure, he points out, that those grandchildren will ask the same time-honored question that so many other generations of curious children have asked: "What did you do in the war, Grandpa?"

What can we tell our children and grandchildren? The thought of looking into those innocent young eyes, and then confessing that we did nothing, is downright frightening — more frightening than a jail term. That fear becomes a powerful motivation to join the pro-life crusade.

However, making a commitment to pro-life work does not necessarily mean joining OR, much less risking arrest. Hundreds of groups fill other essential roles: lobbying for political change, conducting research and issuing reports, setting up shelters for unwed mothers, furnishing homes for needy children — to say nothing of the age-old works of mercy: feeding, clothing, counseling, comforting, and educating those in need. All these works are good works; all these tasks are essential. So why should a busy pro-life activist take on yet another burden, and a risky one at that?

Part of the answer is purely practical. While thousands of people can protect life in hundreds of different ways, *someone* must take a direct stand at the point where the forces of death are strongest. The task of Christians in the world is to shed light. But while so many Christians raise their own candles, *someone* must keep things in perspective by pointing toward the darkness. Anyone who encourages respect for human life is doing God's work, but that work is incomplete unless someone makes the choice abundantly clear by revealing how far *contempt* for human life has filtered into

72

our culture. The abortion industry marks Satan's deepest thrust into American life, the most powerful advance of the forces of death. While many Christians fight valiantly on the flanks, someone must stem that frontal assault.

Lobbying, political campaigning, and legal challenges are certainly essential; without them the pro-life movement cannot expect to change the laws that permit unrestricted abortion on demand. But political work is at best an inexact science. Every pro-life initiative must go into the meat-grinder of debate, deliberation, and amendment before it finally emerges as legislation. Even if the legislation finally passes, and even if the law survives the inevitable court challenges, it might be badly weakened by amendments and compromises; it might be entirely unrecognizable. Again, someone must maintain the perspective of the pro-life movement, reminding lobbyists and political candidates that despite their victories, the slaughter of innocents still continues.

Politics is the art of the possible. Pro-life legislators take small victories wherever they can find them, working at the margins to slow the abortion machinery: restricting government funding for abortion, requiring teenagers to seek their parents' consent, offering information about fetal development, regulating late-term abortions. When those proposals are enacted, the pro-life movement can truly claim important victories; those measures save lives. But they do not address the fundamental question of whether unborn children deserve protection.

On Capitol Hill and in state legislatures around the country, politicians often confuse the issue intentionally to serve their own ambitions. The artificial distinction between someone who is "pro-abortion" and one who is "pro-choice" — a propaganda masterpiece of the abortion industry — has enshrined the confusion. To support "pro-choice" legislation is to ensure that abortion will occur. Pro-choice means pro-abortion. But in the hurly-burly of political campaign rhetoric, that simple logic is elusive. Randall Terry sees a parallel with the campaign against slavery: "Someone who was anti-slavery could believe that slavery was morally wrong, but felt others should be able to own slaves if they wanted," he writes. "On the other hand, what the abolitionists wanted was simple and clear: the immediate, unconditional release of all slaves." OR represents the twentieth-century analog for the abolitionist movement.

Shortly after his presidential inauguration in 1981, President Ronald Reagan called together some of the most influential conservative thinkers in Washington. The conservative movement had been harshly critical of the White House under President Jimmy Carter and was delighted by Reagan's ascendancy. But the new President surprised his old allies by asking them *not* to temper their criticism during his administration. He knew that he would face constant criticism from the political Left, and steady pressure to compromise in that direction. To balance the scales, he explained, "I need pressure from the Right."

On the abortion front, OR provides that unrelenting pressure. Rescuers may not soon win the legislation they seek, but their highly visible actions keep the abortion issue alive in the public debate, forcing politicians to confront the slaughter. OR will accept nothing less than the end to legalized abortion. Knowing that — knowing that a small but determined group will keep fighting for change despite all costs — politicians can never completely forget the unborn. The campaign may take years, but if the pressure is unremitting, the results are inevitable. Again Randall Terry has recognized the political reality and written of it in *Operation Rescue*: "Whether for good or bad, political change comes after a group of Americans bring enough tension in the nation and pressure on the politicians that the laws are changed."

Does that logic work in the practical world of politics? Historians in future generations will look back and decide which American pressure groups contributed most forcefully to the fight against abortion. But even today, the mass media yield their own clues about the practical strength of different pro-life groups. OR is engaged in an "idealistic" sidewalk campaign, not "practical" political lobbying or legal maneuvers. And yet when the media look for a pro-life leader to comment on a new development — even a legislative or legal development — they do not look immediately for the pro-life lobbyists or legal scholars. Their first calls go to Randall Terry.

Hardball politicians should admire Terry's grasp of elementary campaign strategy. But needless to say, the strategy of the Rescue

74

movement is miles removed from ordinary hardball politics. The pressure that OR brings to bear on politicians stems not simply from the movement's persistence but from its powerful moral witness. Week after week, as they sit in front of abortion mills and endure their time in jail, Rescuers prick the nation's conscience, nudging politicians and nonpoliticians alike to reexamine their moral precepts. If the movement continues to grow, or even if it simply endures, more and more ordinary Americans will come into contact with someone who has joined the Rescue crusade. Perhaps it will be a relative or neighbor, perhaps a friend or colleague at work, perhaps only a casual acquaintance. Or perhaps they will happen across the scene when a Rescue takes place. However they come into direct personal contact with the movement, these people will be forced to confront a primal question: Why are these people making this sacrifice? Once they ask themselves that question, Americans will have taken the first step toward a real nationwide campaign against legal abortion. From Broward prison, where she was making her own quiet witness, Joan Andrews encouraged her fellow Rescuers: "All it takes is a very small, but visible and determined, minority willing to suffer and even die for truth and justice in order to force a change."

Up to this point, most dedicated pro-lifers would agree completely with the logic of the Rescue campaign. Yes, we must make a constant, uncompromising stand against all abortion. Yes, we must keep up the pressure. Yes, we must be determined to persevere whatever the costs. On all those points, the pro-life movement can quickly reach unanimous agreement. But OR goes further. Other groups believe that the pro-life movement can work most effectively within the system. OR disagrees. Other groups complain that illegal tactics are counterproductive; they alienate the great mass of people who have not yet made their own personal decisions about abortion. OR disagrees again. Other groups insist that pro-life activists should never disobey the law. On that point, OR disagrees forcefully.

"Should a man or a woman ever break the law?" Randall Terry answers his own question in *Accessory to Murder*: "If that law requires they disobey God, yes! The question, however, really should be framed: 'When man's law and God's law conflict, whom should we obey?' "

Glance back at the abolitionist movement again, and another

intriguing historical precedent leaps into view. The noted preacher Charles Beecher (whose sister Harriet Beecher Stowe made her own massive contribution to the antislavery campaign by writing *Uncle Tom's Cabin*) exhorted his flock against obedience to the fugitive-slave law: "Disobey this law. If you have ever dreamed of obeying it, repent before God, and ask His forgiveness."

Rescuers take a dim view of some American laws, because those laws require Christians to sit by idly and allow the destruction of innocent unborn children. Insofar as they enforce a passive attitude toward abortion, those laws directly contradict God's mandate, which is presented so strongly in the Book of Proverbs (24:11): "Rescue those being dragged to death."

That passage — Proverbs 24:11 — resounds through the Rescue movement. OR leaders are devout Christians with a deep love for the Scriptures; they quote the Bible frequently in their preaching, and even in ordinary conversation. But no other passage is quoted as frequently as that one. OR participants wear T-shirts emblazoned with it; it serves as the subtitle for Randall Terry's book *Operation Rescue*. Ask Rescuers where they receive permission to defy the law, and they will turn immediately to the Book of Proverbs, repeating the familiar refrain: "Rescue those being dragged to death." The Rescue movement exists to fulfill that command.

God's law mandates a rescue. Man's law — whether it is a federal law or a state regulation, a local statute or a court injunction — forbids any such action. The two are incompatible. So what should earnest Christians do? Terry quotes Brother Andrew, who for many years routinely broke the local laws of Eastern Europe by smuggling Bibles and Christian religious books across the borders. In his autobiographical book *God's Smuggler*, Brother Andrew referred all questions back to the Acts of the Apostles. Brought before the Sanhedrin to explain why he had continued to preach — in violation of his own legal authorities — St. Peter answered boldly: "Obedience before God comes before obedience to men. . ." (Acts 5:29).

(Another verse with a special significance for OR occurs a few verses later in that same chapter of Acts. When asked if he was sure that OR was God's will, Bishop Austin Vaughan harked back to the wisdom of Gamaliel, the Pharisee who intervened with the Sanhedrin on Peter's behalf. If OR is not the work of the Holy Spirit, Bishop Vaughan reasoned, it will soon die of its own weakness; if it *is* God's will, its success is assured.)

So Christian theology provides a clear answer. But so does our own country's legal tradition. In the building that houses the Pennsylvania Supreme Court, the walls are inscribed with a quotation from Blackstone, whose *Commentaries* furnish the acknowledged definitive source of the Anglo-American common-law tradition. "The Law of Nature dictated by God Himself is superior to any other. It is binding over all the globe, in all countries and at all times. No human laws are of any validity if contrary to this, and such of them as are valid derive their force and all their authority mediately and immediately from this original. Upon these two foundations, the Law of Nature and the Law of Revelation, depend all human laws."

Human law changes; the laws of Nature and of Nature's God do not. So whatever legal problems they face today, Rescuers retain courage in the assurance that their trials will eventually cease and their righteousness will be rewarded. Shortly before he was sentenced to serve thirty months in prison for violating a state court injunction, Bill Cotter of OR-Boston could still wisecrack: "Judge Lauriat has made his injunction permanent . . . or so he *thinks*."

That attitude, so comforting to Rescue activists, can be equally frustrating to court officials. The American judicial system handles thousands of trials every day, but virtually every defendant comes before the court as a humble petitioner. If the evidence weighs against the defendant, he usually shows signs of sorrow — even if it is feigned sorrow — for his transgressions. Judges are accustomed to seeing at least the pretext of repentance on the part of defendants, and a lively deference from their lawyers. But Rescue defendants challenge the court directly, looking judges in the eye and telling them that *they*, the *judges*, are the ones on trial! That approach infuriates some judges. As he did so often during Wichita's historic summer of 1991, Judge Patrick Kelly set the standard for irascible conduct, with an outburst at Randall Terry: "Your soul may belong to God, but your butt belongs to me, and you're going to jail!"

Despite the judges' ire, the calm self-assurance of Rescue leaders (like the phenomenon Mark Twain dubbed "the quiet confidence of a Christian holding four aces") pricks again at American consciences. Even in an essay bitterly attacking OR, published in *The Nation*, Philip Green coughed up a grudging recognition of the moral challenge: "Who can argue with this 'sincerity'? Still, we must argue or we will be victimized by the kind of guilt . . ." that OR makes the pro-abortion lobby feel.

Earnest Christians can cite many good, sound, logical reasons why they should avoid contact with OR, and especially with the illegal activities that might earn them a jail sentence. We all have children to raise, careers to pursue, bills to pay, assignments to complete. These are all solid, responsible arguments. But OR leader Joseph Foreman raises a warning finger. Pregnant women, he notes, cite those same solid, logical reasons when they abort their babies. They cannot afford to interrupt their careers, they say; they cannot afford the financial strain; they cannot afford the emotional toll on their families. In short, the reasons some pro-lifers cite to justify their passivity mirror the reasons some women cite to justify their abortions. In both cases, too many people are simply unwilling to make a sacrifice on behalf of human life.

Foreman asks his audience to answer a startling question. When they are aborted, will these unborn children go to heaven or hell? If they have souls, those souls must eventually abide in one place or another; where? Whichever way the audience answers, Foreman can cite a formidable challenge, based on the Gospel of St. Matthew.

If the baby's souls are destined for hell, Foreman points out, then the Christian community has utterly failed to fulfill the mission which Jesus gave to his followers (Matthew 28:19): "Go, therefore, make disciples of all nations" The number of unborn Americans killed by abortion now outstrips the population of many of the world's nations. Yet here, in the midst of a country where eighty-seven percent of the population is nominally Christian, we have done nothing to preach the Gospel to these souls. If the unborn children had heard the news of salvation preached to them — even if they had felt the message of love enacted on the streets by Christians trying to save their lives — then perhaps American Christians could accept their fate peacefully. But they have not heard the Gospel; we have failed.

The overwhelming majority of Christians, however, believe that the innocent unborn children will find their way to heaven, to become brothers and sisters of Christ in the fullest sense. That is certainly good news for the babies, Foreman agrees, but it is not a thought that should ease the Christian conscience. If we believe that they are going to heaven, then we must prepare to meet our own final judgment, which was so vividly pictured by Jesus Himself in Matthew's Gospel (25:40): "Insofar as you did this to one of these, the least of my brethren, you did it for me." Who could more aptly be described as the least of Christ's brethren, if not the helpless unborn? We knew that they were facing a painful death; we knew that they were the cherished brothers and sisters of the Lord Himself. And we stood by? Then we should not sleep easily.

Summing up the question in *Newsday*, a distinctly unsympathetic B.D. Colen wrote, "Anyone who believes that abortion is murder has a moral obligation to join Operation Rescue. How can they not?"

Actually, not even the most ardent OR recruiter would claim that every pro-life Christian should join the ranks of sidewalk activists. Yes, every Christian is obligated to fight against abortion, but the exact form of that fight might differ from one person to another. We each have our special talents, our special limitations, and our special vocation. OR needs volunteers who are willing to risk arrest, Randall Terry emphasizes, just as any army needs plenty of front-line troops. But armies need different units as well. The individual's exact strategic role is not important; the crucial point is to enlist.

After prayerful reflection, many sincere pro-life Christians honestly believe that they are not called to risk arrest. If so, OR leaders unhesitatingly tell them, they should certainly not join the blockades. On the other hand some Rescuers feel called to venture even beyond that point. Writing from her jail cell to Joseph Foreman, Joan Andrews revealed that her "noncooperation" policy was based on the private appeals of her own conscience: "It would not be objectively immoral for me to cooperate in prison because to cooperate here is much removed from the actual killing. But the reason it would be immoral for me to cooperate at this point is that I do believe God has asked me to take this stand."

In the abortion conflict as in any other, the most important battles are the struggles that individuals work out privately, within the dictates of their own conscience. Joseph Foreman asks Christians to remember the advice that Mordecai gave to Esther: God will surely save the people of Israel; the question is whether He will save your own house. Similarly today, God will surely bring an eventual end to the violent injustice of abortion. The question for us — for each individual Christian — is not whether we can stop abortion by our own human efforts, but whether we will answer God's call. God will save the babies. Will we save ourselves?

A faithful few can inspire the participation of others, and their suffering may fertilize the ground that others will harvest. God's work flourishes on earth when Christians shoulder the load and bear their burden faithfully. In March 1987, Joan Andrews wrote to pro-life leaders from prison: "If the price to be paid became higher, I think our numbers would swell. But only if the few now remain resolute, and suffer the consequences first."

No one knows the end of the American story. No one knows when, or how, the scourge of abortion will be lifted. No one knows whether OR will ultimately succeed or fail in its goal of stopping the Holocaust. But ultimately even that question is irrelevant. Randall Terry sums up:

> "When people ask after a rescue whether we achieved our goal, it is hard to answer. Most of the babies usually die after we are removed. Not all of them, but most of them. Were we trying to save a few? Absolutely not — we were trying to save all the babies scheduled to die there that day. Well, then, does that mean we failed? No, because we were really trying to be obedient to the Lord, who asked us to rescue those babies. And if we were obedient, then the results are in God's hands, not ours."

6

The Faithful Remnant

RESCUE LEADERS joined the battle in the face of tremendous odds, confident that God would reward their work. Many other prominent Christians, speaking with equal certitude, denounced the Rescue movement as misguided or even sinful. The ensuing debate caused some real friction among Evangelical congregations, and within the Roman Catholic Church.

Rescue leaders were prepared for criticism from the more liberal Protestant denominations, especially from the churches which expressed support for legal abortion. Although sociologists might combine all American Christians into one religious category, in practice the mainline denominations are separated from the more conservative Evangelical and Catholic groups by a steadily growing theological gulf. Rescuers expected opposition from liberal Christians, and they were not disappointed. The Religious Coalition for Abortion Rights mobilized ministers to appear on television news programs condemning the blockades. Catholics for A Free Choice, an organization which is clearly outside the pale of the Catholic Church, incessantly repeated its absurd contention that abortion is sometimes acceptable within the Catholic tradition. Some Protestant churches teamed with the clinics, offering their buildings as "staging areas" for clinics affected by blockades. In Wichita, at the height of the "Summer of Mercy," the abortionist Dr. Tiller announced that his religious faith and the support expressed by members of his own parish had given him strength to continue his work.

Viewed through the eyes of Operation Rescue, all that opposition was grotesque but predictable. OR leaders, however, were caught off guard, and often personally hurt, by the strong and sometimes vituperative opposition they encountered among the conservative Christians they had hoped to count among their allies.

Roussas Rushdoony, a Christian preacher with a nationwide following, expressed his condemnation in sweeping terms when he commented on clinic blockades: "The methodology of such demonstrations has been borrowed from non-Christian and revolutionary sources. From one end of the Bible to the other, no warrant can be found for this methodology."

If by "methodology" he meant the tactics of OR, then Rev. Rushdoony's point is at least partially accurate. The early pioneers of the Rescue movement had acknowledged their debt to Mahatma Mohandas K. Gandhi, a non-Christian exponent of nonviolent activism. But then Gandhi in turn had been heavily influenced by Christian thought. And Pope John Paul II had told American pro-life leaders, "In these matters, I take Mahatma Gandhi as my mentor." Surely nonviolent resistance is not incompatible with Christian faith. If they learned tactical lessons from non-Christian sources, Rescuers were certainly not abandoning their Christian principles.

But the second count of Rev. Rushdoony's indictment — that no warrant could be found in the Bible to justify Rescues — struck OR leaders as almost unbelievably wrongheaded. The Scriptures teem with stories of righteous people who defied the authorities of their community. Elijah destroyed the idols of Baal. The Maccabees revolted against an unjust king. St. Peter continued preaching the Gospel despite a series of injunctions. From the Old Testament to the New, and from the early days of Christianity up to the present, the Church has celebrated thousands of righteous men and women who have defied public authorities in order to serve God's will.

Ah, but what is God's will? Doesn't the Bible enjoin Christians to obey the law at all times? Critics of OR pointed to the thirteenth chapter of St. Paul's epistle to the Romans: "Everyone is to obey the governing authorities, because there is no authority except from God and so whatever authorities exist have been appointed by God. So anyone who disobeys an authority is rebelling against God's ordinance."

In *Accessory to Murder*, Randall Terry made a devastating response to that argument: "I would point out that the author of Romans 13 also wrote four prison epistles."

Back and forth the argument flew, with both critics and supporters of the Rescue movement finding scriptural support for their positions. Randall Terry's book *Operation Rescue* is largely devoted to the task of providing a solid justification for the Rescue movement, based on the Bible and drawn from the lessons of Church history. Randy Alcorn's *Is Rescuing Right?* concentrates exclusively on that same assignment. Each book cites literally dozens of precedents to support the essential point: that Christians are not obligated to obey — and may be obligated to disobey — an unjust law.

The American legal system allows abortion on demand, and that situation is unjust. But during OR's 1988 siege of Atlanta, the leaders of that city's First Baptist Church issued a highly publicized statement, based on "prayerful and carefully studied view of the pastoral staff and deacons", which drew a careful distinction between laws that allowed abortion and a law that would require abortion. If the law required abortion, the statement concluded, then Christians would be justified in breaking the law. But since the law merely allowed women to make their own moral choice, Rescue tactics were not justifiable. That public rebuke was a serious blow for OR, particularly because Rev. Charles Stanley, the pastor of First Baptist, was also a former president of the Southern Baptist Association; a statement put forth by his congregation was guaranteed a wide acceptance among members of that denomination. Naturally, pro-abortion advocates were delighted with the development; Kate Michelman of the National Abortion Rights Action League loudly applauded the Baptist statement.

Essentially the same argument would pop up repeatedly in criticisms of the Rescue movement. During OR's most successful recruiting drive, throughout 1989, the influential evangelist John McArthur persisted in his critique of OR with a series of radio messages, complaining, "you are penalizing the government for something that is really not their authorization." And late in 1991, Boston's Catholic Cardinal Bernard Law wrote that while he admired the courage of Rescuers, he could not personally recommend civil disobedience. The laws that Rescuers defy — laws against trespassing, or obstructing public sidewalks, or disobeying a judge's order — are not themselves unjust laws, the Cardinal wrote; they do not deserve defiance.

Once again, OR leaders have a reply. Rescuers do not trespass in day-care centers, nor do they block access to fast-food restaurants. Under ordinary circumstances, trespassing is immoral, and laws that prohibit it are just laws. But the circumstances that obtain at an abortion clinic are far from ordinary. The tactics of the Rescue movement cannot be divorced from their goal.

Imagine that in an isolated village, suffering from a terrible famine, one man owned a storehouse crammed with food. If that man refused to share his food with his starving neighbors, wouldn't they be justified in breaking into his storehouse? The laws that protect private property are important, but they are not absolute. In the tradition of Catholic social teaching, scholars speak of a "social mortgage" on property; ownership carries responsibilities, and anyone who grossly violates those responsibilities undercuts his moral right to hold that property. In Nazi Germany, presumably the commandants of the death camps held a proper legal title to the buildings that housed the gas chambers. And again, the laws protecting private property are not unjust laws. But if Christian saboteurs had destroyed those buildings, would anyone today question the morality of their actions?

Unfortunately, the death camps of the Third Reich remained intact until the end of World War II. And to this day, critics ask why the Christian churches of Europe did not do more to stop the Holocaust. Much of that criticism is unfair and uninformed; many righteous Christians valiantly fought to save the lives of Jews and others condemned by the Nazi regime. Yet the fact remains that the overwhelming majority of professed Christians did nothing to stop the Holocaust.

Rescue leaders beg American Christians not to be guilty of the same passivity in the face of our nation's own Holocaust. Relatively few Americans are directly implicated in the abortion industry. But even passive acceptance of the killing is unconscionable. In *Accessory to Murder*, Randall Terry quotes Martin Luther: "If you see anyone condemned to death innocently and you do not save him, although you know ways and means to do so, you have killed him. It will do you no good to plead that you did not contribute to his death, for you have withheld your love from him and have robbed him of the service by which his life might have been saved."

Why have the American churches been so silent in the face of the abortion industry? That question haunts OR leaders. The fabric of our society has been shredded — not only by abortion, but also by the widespread acceptance of homosexuality, pornography, drug

Rescue in progress: Pro-life activists blockade a New York abortion clinic during the week-long Rescues held there in early May of 1988.

Prayerful witness: Although they do not participate in physical blockades, or risk arrest, "prayer supporters" are essential to the Rescue effort.

Sidewalk counseling: With or without the help of a blockade, pro-lifers outside the abortuaries offer pregnant women information, advice, and help.

Passive resistance: Rescuers are instructed to let themselves fall limp when they are arrested, forcing police to carry them bodily away from abortuaries. The extra seconds they buy might mean another "save."

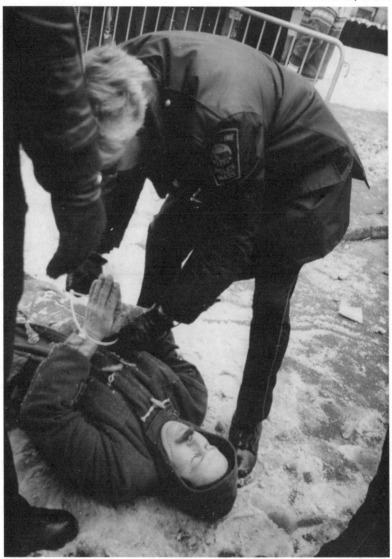

Above: Supine prayer position in passive resistance. Opposite, at top, "The Crawl": Inching forward on hands and knees — in an inherently non-threatening posture — Rescuers force police to lean over to stop them. Below, "Lockdown": With a chain of bicycle locks around their necks, Rescuers can't be moved without a locksmith or literally risking lives.

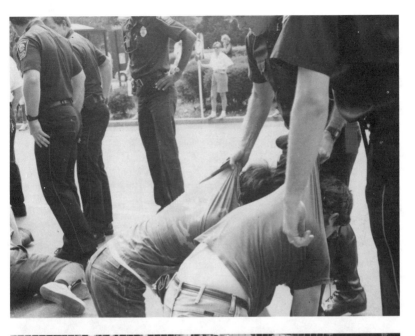

Sidewalk confrontation: Police outside the clinics must often serve a dual role, protecting pro-lifers from hostile pro-abortion demonstrators.

Above: Confrontation. Below: Sidewalk booking. Police usually photograph and fingerprint arrested Rescuers in local stations, but after arresting over 100 Cleveland pro-lifers they set up a streetside processing system.

Roadblocks: Federal marshals, ordered by Judge Patrick Kelly, remove Rescuers lying in the road to stop cars entering a Wichita abortuary.

Above: Wichita. Hundreds of pro-lifers prayed outside City Hall during the peak of OR's Summer of Mercy campaign in 1991. Below: Hope for the Heartland. Thirty thousand exuberant pro-lifers jammed a local football stadium for the rally that climaxed the Kansas town's Summer of Mercy.

Richard Bruck photo © 1981

Above: Joe Scheidler, the godfather of pro-life direct-action campaigns, with trademark hat and bullhorn. Below: Joan Andrews. After two years in prison, often in solitary confinement, the pro-life heroine emerges from Allegheny County Jail in October 1988, surrounded by well-wishers.

CNS photo by John C. Keenan, *Pittsburgh Catholic*

Randall Terry: Operation Rescue's dynamic founder preaches his practices.

CNS photo by Charles F. Sibre, *The Catholic Standard and Times*

Reuters photo, Bettmann Archive

Above: Bishop Austin Vaughn chats with clerks at Chester County (Pa.) Jail before serving a two-day sentence for Rescue activities. Right: Federal Judge Patrick Kelly. In Wichita, his emotional reaction to the Rescue movement lent special urgency to the Summer of Mercy.

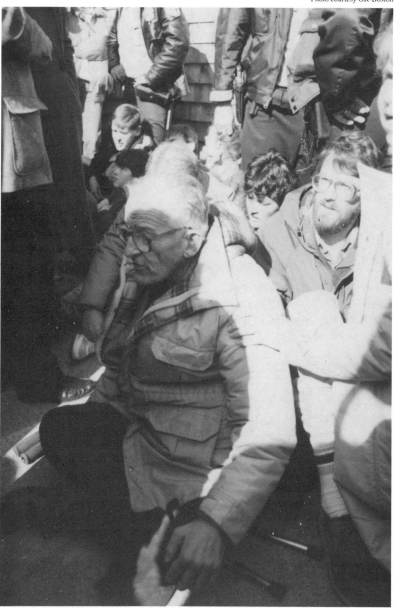

Dr. Joseph Stanton. Sitting on his crutches, the senior statesman of America's pro-life movement awaits arrest outside a Boston abortuary.

Above: Bill Cotter. Defying a court injunction the head of OR-Boston surveys his "troops" before giving the order to begin a blockade. Below: The author (foreground, in knit cap) links arms with fellow Rescuers outside a Planned Parenthood clinic in Brookline, Mass., March 1991.

abuse, adultery, and a host of other evils. Yet for the most part, the churches have been content to minister to their own flocks.

What will it take to energize Christians and thrust them into the battle to restore our society? Randall Terry asks a church audience to think back a generation. Imagine that a speaker had come before a congregation in the same church in 1960, and accurately predicted the conditions that face us in 1990. Terry recites a litany of the horrors that speaker might have included among his predictions: 1.5 million unborn children are legally executed each year; condoms are freely available in public schools, but prayer is banned; pornographic movies are subsidized by government grants; and so forth. If anyone had predicted these developments back in 1960, Terry points out, his audience would have dismissed him as a lunatic. Now Terry challenges his audience directly. What do you suppose will happen in the next thirty years? Do you have any reason to doubt that the moral decay will continue — and probably even accelerate? If Christians do not stop the momentum now, he concludes, their churches cannot expect to survive in the climate of the year 2020. Worse still, if the churches do not take action now, they will not *deserve* to survive.

The churches have been quiet too long, Terry concludes, and now American Christianity desperately needs a vigorous public renewal. In *Accessory to Murder* he recalls the prophet Nehemiah, whose witness reformed the Hebrew society of his day. But the abuses uprooted by Nehemiah were trivial in comparison with our society's woes; "what got Nehemiah so angry couldn't hold a candle to some of the atrocities we face in our nation." When he founded Operation Rescue, Terry had no doubt about the first step toward success: "First of all, we needed a repentance in the Church."

OR is not only a pro-life organization, then; it is also — even principally — a movement for reform within the Christian churches. In a brochure advertising his Missionaries to the Pre-Born, Joseph Foreman lists: "His Goal: Revival in the Church."

Foreman, too, asks a church audience to hark back to 1960. He portrays an imaginary conference held in heaven that year, in which Satan recounts all his successes in fomenting evil throughout the world. But God counters by pointing to the Christian churches of America: rich, flourishing, busy, vocal — churches that supported an extraordinarily high level of religious practice and charitable works. But Satan admits nothing. Those Christians are not practicing because they love *you*, he tells God; they just love all the blessings you have poured out upon them. Give them a bit of adversity — give them a society that gradually becomes hostile to Christian faith; give them a country that allows systematic killing of the unborn — and see how those Christians react. Will they remain loyal to God? Or will they hedge their bets, protecting their social standing by avoiding a head-on confrontation with moral corruption?

Foreman himself, obviously, believes that American Christians have chosen the latter route, forsaking their faith. If that judgment seems harsh, keep in mind that Foreman has painful memories of his own — memories of being abandoned by most of the Christian community. The Foreman family lives in Atlanta, a city that is home to about two thousand Christian churches. Yet when Foreman went to prison, to serve a sentence he incurred by refusing to compromise the principles of his own faith, those churches did not rally to his support. There were no massive protest marches, no campaigns to mount pressure on the prison authorities. There were not even church-based charitable efforts to ensure that the Foreman children would have enough to eat while their father was in jail; his wife was forced to rely on the local food pantry.

Why have the churches not rallied to support OR? Why have Christian denominations — which teach that abortion is the deliberate extinction of human life — continued with business as usual while the abortion industry roars along in high gear? Rescue leaders worry that much of the problem can be traced to fear: fear of alienating some marginal church members, fear of losing tax exemptions, fear of political reprisals, fear of a decline in contributions.

Randall Terry admits that those fears are realistic. If the Christian community launches an all-out assault on the abortion industry, that powerful industry will surely fight back. But if that is the price of Christian witness, so be it. Terry points out that the Scriptures *guarantee* trials and torments for faithful Christians. And a small dose of oppression might do wonders to awaken the dormant faith of America's Christians: "What revival would take place if the churches were filled with joyful testimonies of Christians being persecuted for standing for what is right! The fact is, we are probably doing something wrong if we are *not* persecuted."

In some churches where the congregation has become deeply involved in the Rescue movement, Terry's predictions have been fulfilled. The pastor of a small Evangelical church in Boston reports that when he first become involved with OR, prominent members of his congregation warned him that he might suffer adverse financial consequences. He continued his involvement, and now he does face a major financial problem, but it is not at all the sort of problem his critics had in mind. Today he must find the money to build a new parking lot, to accommodate all the people who have begun flocking into his church every Sunday morning!

That example is far from typical, however. Bill Cotter of OR-Boston laments, "You can hardly find a clergyman anywhere who takes this as an important issue — nowhere near the urgency as if the church building fell down, or even an apartment building in the area." Children are dying — right down the street from the churches that preach against abortion. "In some ways, the church's guilt is as bad as that of the abortionist," Randall Terry writes. "Why? Because the church could have stopped this holocaust by now. We have the mandate, the manpower, and the money."

How can OR turn the tide? Terry inspires his audiences by recalling the prophets and reformers of the Old Testament. As long as there is a faithful remnant in Israel, God will guide His people to victory. Operation Rescue is the faithful remnant among the American Christian people. In a nation marred by corruption, where religious leaders have forsaken their public duties, the Rescue movement sees itself as an instrument of religious revival.

Even in their harshest critiques of Christian passivity, Rescue leaders acknowledge that the Catholic church has been forceful and consistent in its public stance against abortion, from the time before *Roe v. Wade* up until the present. But that very intense public involvement has tempted Catholic leaders to concentrate on the political aspects of the issue, rather than the need for unalloyed Christian witness. When the Rescue movement first began to take root in St. Louis, Archbishop John May wholeheartedly opposed it; he even castigated the "lawbreakers" at a time when no one involved in the Rescues had been convicted of any crime. His preference for an indirect political approach exhausted the patience of Joan Andrews, who complained bitterly that the archbishop "would talk only about the 'issue' of abortion, about public relations and turning people off and breaking the law and all this technical stuff, when little babies were about to be torn apart."

Archbishop May encouraged the police officers of St. Louis to enforce the law and arrest the Rescuers. But again his argument was based on the need for public order, not the objective rights of the unborn. Several years later, when a devout Catholic policeman from Corpus Christi asked Bishop René Gracida for advice on the same question, Bishop Gracida offered a clear example of Catholic moral teaching: "When a police officer removes the last obstacles preventing the murder of a child, by moving rescuers from the doorway, he becomes a party to the horrible act. Anyone who physically assists the abortionist in this way indirectly participates in the killing." By that time, several Catholic bishops had joined in Rescue blockades, with one — Bishop Austin Vaughan — ranked as one of the movement's most popular public speakers.

Catholics in the Rescue movement were repeatedly baffled, and sometimes felt thoroughly betrayed, by the political logic of some bishops. But an even greater problem stemmed from the religious logic of politicians. Many Catholic elected officials, eager to prove that they were not taking orders from Rome, voted consistently in favor of legalized abortion, while insisting that they were "personally opposed" to the practice. Catholic prosecutors and judges, equally eager to avoid any appearance of favoritism, went to the other extreme. Again Joan Andrews (herself a fiercely loyal and devout Catholic) summed up the frustration:

> ". . . when we go into court and get a Catholic judge, usually we expect the worst. The judge will probably lean over backward to prove that his legal decisions are not influenced by his 'sectarian beliefs.' To prove it, he will nail us. Over and over, Catholic judges insist all through a trial that abortion is not the issue, that the issue is just trespass or whatever. 'I do not want to hear your philosophy or any emotional feelings,' they all say. But then when the trial is over, and they have spent all that time telling us to be quiet about abortion, it comes time for

sentencing. And all of a sudden, the issue is 'privacy' or 'pluralism' or 'the American way' or some other philosophical, emotion-laden concept. With Catholic judges, we are tried for trespass, but we get sentenced for treason, bigotry, abusing women, everything."

No judge played that role more forcefully than Patrick Kelly in Wichita's federal court. Patrick Monaghan, a lawyer who represented OR defendants in Kelly's court, recalls: "He described himself as a Roman Catholic judge. I felt like saying to him, 'Well, Henry VIII was a Roman Catholic king.' "

Henry VIII crushed the Catholic Church in England. Judge Kelly worked overtime to crush Operation Rescue, and in doing so he worked assiduously to extinguish the remains of his own Catholic moral training, argues Monaghan — who adds that the most fascinating sub-plot of the Wichita drama was Kelly's "public wrestling with his conscience, which nobody caught onto. . . ."

Indeed, a good deal of that wrestling took place in plain view. Judge Kelly reported that he had stopped attending Mass in his parish church because so many of his fellow parishioners were vehement pro-lifers. (He thereby confirmed a friend's report, quoted by *The New York Times*, that he was "a judge first and a Catholic second.") When a nun appeared before him in court, he illustrated his alienation from his Catholic faith with an apparently inadvertent choice of words, saying, "I pray for the day when I hear *your* church leaders say [that Rescuers should obey the law]." (Emphasis added.)

Yet as Monaghan suggests, Judge Kelly could not seem to get the Catholic church off his mind. He repeatedly chided Bishop Eugene Gerber for failing to stop the blockades, although Catholics certainly did not dominate — or even exercise leadership — in the Rescue contingent active in Wichita. (Monaghan cracked, "I felt like there were nine Catholics in Wichita, and when [his partner] Walter and I left there would be seven.") Of the OR leaders prominent in the Summer of Mercy campaign (Randall Terry, Keith Tucci, Patrick Mahoney, Michael McMonagle, Joseph Foreman, Joseph Slovenic) only McMonagle is Catholic — and he, ironically, is the only OR leader who never locked horns with Judge Kelly in the Wichita courtroom.

The earliest ancestors of Operation Rescue were indeed dominated by Catholics. Joe Scheidler, John Ryan, Joe Wall, Joan Andrews, Juli Loesch, and John Cavanaugh-O'Keefe are all Catholics. But even as early as the St. Louis campaign, the movement expanded to accommodate a group of Evangelical activists, who had been heavily influenced by Francis Schaeffer's powerful statement against abortion in *Whatever Happened to the Human Race?* (with C. Everett Koop, Good News [Crossway Books], 1983). From that time on, the two main groups — Catholics and Evangelicals — have flourished together in Rescue activities.

What is the secret of this ecumenical success? In part, OR is marked by the respect its members share for fellow-Rescuers of different Christian denominations. Randall Terry is unusually knowledgeable about Catholic beliefs; Joan Andrews is delighted to share a jailhouse prayer with Evangelical friends. "Most Protestants think I'm Catholic," shrugs Joseph Foreman, an ordained Presbyterian minister, who peppers his preaching with good-humored but pointed parodies ("inter-faithless jokes," he calls them) of different denominational peculiarities. Far more important, Catholic and Evangelical Rescuers alike can agree on their religious duty to protect unborn children, and to call for reform within the Christian Church.

If they examined their theological differences carefully, Catholics and Evangelicals might find a wide gulf separating them. But in the Rescue movement they set aside those differences, to unite for a purpose both groups can wholeheartedly endorse. Now and then an ill-considered phrase can strain ecumenical sensibilities, but the remarkable unity of the Rescue movement has survived despite those trials. Rescues might begin with separate church services: Mass for Catholics, a prayer meeting for Evangelicals. And on the site of the Rescue, different groups occasionally peel off from the crowd to pray in their own fashion; typically, Catholics pray the Rosary together apart from the ecumenical crowd. But OR leaders of both groups can agree in choosing hymns, take turns in leading prayers, and adopt a compromise version of the Lord's Prayer.

Looking out over an audience of thirty-five thousand who had flocked to the Hope for the Heartland rally in Wichita, George Grant assessed the results of this practical ecumenism: "The lesson of

Wichita is that when grandmoms in tennis shoes and nuns saying their rosaries and charismatics singing praise songs and pastors and deacons gather together peacefully on a sidewalk to resist the ripping to shreds of real innocent children, that all the powerful forces of our nation tremble with fear."

In a nation where eighty-seven percent of all citizens identify themselves as Christians, the continued spread of the abortion culture stands as a devastating indictment of the churches in the minds of Rescue leaders. Operation Rescue proposes to close down the abortion clinics, but even if it is successful, that action will not eradicate the moral stain on American culture. OR hopes to take one crucial step further, sparking a new burst of public Christian witness in our society. Randall Terry sees a clear agenda for the organization he founded: "Scripture warns and history proves that when the church is not on the offensive — by walking in faith, holiness, and obedience — not only does she not take ground, she loses it."

7

The Media's Blind Spot

NUTRITIONISTS SAY we are what we eat. Computer programmers have their own pithy expression to explain why faulty data always yield faulty results: garbage in, garbage out.

The same fundamental insight applies to public opinion. If the mass media ignore an issue, or if their stories persistently distort the facts, then their audience cannot form an educated opinion on that issue. Any blindness or prejudice that infects the media will inevitably spread to the public at large.

Media bias comes in two different forms. The first, more blatant sort of distortion involves the intentional slanting of stories: using loaded adjectives, painting favorable or unfavorable portraits, tailoring quotations, manipulating the facts to fit the reporter's own personal agenda. The second form of distortion is more difficult to detect — in fact, journalists themselves might be quite unaware of the prejudices they harbor — but in the long run it is even more important. This second type of bias involves the selection of topics.

News coverage always entails a series of judgments; reporters must choose which stories are most important or most interesting, which facts are most salient, and which sources are most credible. Editors must decide which reports deserve top billing and which news events deserve the greatest coverage. Which story should be on the newspaper's front page? Which videotape should be shown at the top of the evening's newscast? These are all subjective judgments.

Successful journalists learn to make those editorial judgments carefully, balancing their own personal instincts, the views of their colleagues, and the responses they hear from members of their audience. Good reporters constantly search for their own new and provocative stories, but even the most ambitious reporters need some professional encouragement. It takes real independence for a reporter to keep digging for details when others have abandoned the story. But it takes much more independence — in fact, it demands real personal courage — to risk a journalistic career by pursuing a story that other journalists consider boring, irrelevant, or distasteful.

The overwhelming majority of American journalists regard the pro-life movement as boring, or distasteful, or both. Moreover, that hostility to the pro-life movement is most pronounced among the journalists who exercise the greatest influence within their profession.

In 1985, a *New York Times* poll found that eighty-five percent of all reporters supported legalized abortion. That overwhelming percentage by itself is remarkable. But further studies, concentrating more precisely on the leading practitioners of journalism, yielded even more one-sided results. A 1986 poll by the Center for Media and Public Affairs, surveying reporters from the nation's top ten media outlets, found that ninety percent supported a woman's legal right to choose abortion. The trend among top younger journalists suggested an even stronger bias: in the 1982 graduating class at the prestigious Columbia Journalism School, ninety-six percent embraced the "pro-choice" position.

On the corporate level, the world of journalism is dominated by the same strong pro-abortion bias. The corporations which publish *The New York Times*, *The Washington Post*, *Los Angeles Times*, *The Boston Globe*, *Newsday*, and *USA Today* all contribute to NOW, Planned Parenthood, and/or the Women's Legal Defense Fund. At a 1989 convention the Newspaper Guild, the reporters' union, strongly endorsed legalized abortion.

Opposition to abortion usually stems from religious conviction. Here, too, the personal lives of elite journalists are far removed from the American mainstream. The Center for Media and Public Affairs revealed that only fifty percent maintained any religious affiliation, with just thirty-three percent professing to be Christians. (By contrast, in the American public at large, fully ninety percent of the people maintain a religious affiliation, and eighty-seven percent are Christians.) Only eight percent of the elite journalists attend weekly worship services, and eighty-six percent rarely enter a church building.

The pro-life movement organizes around Christian churches. Reporters rarely see the inside of those churches. It follows that reporters rarely see — or understand — pro-lifers in action. From the perspective of mainstream American journalism, pro-life organizations are like mysterious foreign nations: exotic, inscrutable, and perhaps a bit frightening.

Like all normal human beings, journalists are inclined to favor the arguments which they themselves support. So it should not be surprising if the mass media show a preference for the "pro-choice" side of the abortion issue — and the more influential the media outlet, the more likely that news coverage will emphasize those arguments. At the same time, because they are largely untouched by religious affiliations, journalists are less likely to recognize the religious arguments against abortion, or to be personally acquainted with people who cherish those arguments.

The result is a persistent prejudice among journalists in favor of legal abortion. Ethan Bronner of *The Boston Globe* summed it up simply: "Opposing abortion, in the eyes of most journalists, is not a legitimate, civilized position in our society. I think that when abortion opponents complain about a bias in the newsrooms against their cause, they're right."

In July 1990, David Shaw, the Pulitzer-prizewinning media critic of the *Los Angeles Times*, published a massive four-part study of how journalists have handled the abortion controversy. Although the *Times* itself has a clear "pro-choice" editorial policy, Shaw's survey was crisp and professional. He found and scrupulously documented a vivid pattern of prejudice against the pro-life movement; journalists showed an unmistakable tendency to use the language of abortion supporters, to quote abortion advocates more frequently, to ignore pro-life events and arguments, and even to distort the analysis of public events, such as election results. By Shaw's tabulation, editorial columnists favoring legalized abortion outnumber pro-life writers by more than two to one in the nation's leading newspapers.

Although Shaw backed his argument with scores of examples and quotations, one incident stands out. In April 1989, a few weeks prior to the Supreme Court's public decision in the landmark *Webster* case, over two hundred thousand demonstrators came to Washington to support legal abortion. The hometown *Washington Post* provided massive coverage of the event: five different stories leading up to the march, with an exhaustive five-story, three-picture, 7,000-word extravaganza on the day following the event. The following April, over two hundred thousand marchers came to

Washington to *protest* legal abortion. The *Post* provided one single short story, on the day following the march, in the paper's Metro section. Richard Harwood of the *Post* sheepishly explained that his reporters simply were not aware of the importance of the pro-life march; no one on the *Post* staff was acquainted with the marchers or their ideas.

Although David Shaw's research provided compelling proof of a pro-abortion bias in the media, other evidence abounds. Can anyone really believe it was a pure coincidence that NBC aired "Roe v. Wade," a made-for-TV movie with a clear "pro-choice" message, in May 1989, just as the nation waited for a Supreme Court ruling in the pivotal *Webster* case? Time and again, journalists have ignored or downplayed stories that might help the pro-life cause, while emphasizing those that would tend to support legalized abortion.

● Like most loosely regulated industries, the abortion business is subject to widespread abuse. Pro-life activists accuse abortionists of offering unsanitary conditions, rushed treatment, and haphazard follow-up on any post-abortion medical complaints. In 1978, an investigative team from the *Chicago Sun-Times* found such corruption widespread among the area's abortion clinics; one reporter was scheduled for an "abortion" although she was not pregnant! (As a historical footnote, many of the nation's laws restricting abortion can be traced to a pioneering investigative series in *The New York Times*, which exposed the horrors of illegal abortion mills back in 1871.) Since that time, investigative reporters have ignored the abortion industry — although, in the Chicago area alone, 145 women have filed malpractice suits against abortionists during the last 20 years.

● In 1990 the attorney general of Illinois, Neal Hartigan, agreed to an out-of-court settlement in the *Ragsdale* case. Since that case involved the state's new restrictive abortion law, and since Hartigan was a candidate for governor at the time, most reporters cited this episode as a political victory for the "pro-choice" movement. Only Nina Tottenberg, who covers the Supreme Court for National Public Radio, saw another dimension to the issue. This, she reported, was the first instance she could recall in which a state attorney general tried to avoid an appearance before the Supreme Court. Hartigan's decision was an astonishing one. But the meaning of his unprecedented act was lost amid the cheerleading for a perceived pro-choice victory.

● In July 1990, when over two hundred pro-life activists were jailed in West Hartford, Connecticut, *The New York Times* completely ignored their arrest. *Times* readers only learned about the massive arrests several days later, in a story about crowding in the area's prisons. Consider that editorial judgment: the overcrowding was worthy of coverage, yet the massive arrests which precipitated that crowding were not!

● Abortion is the most common elective surgical procedure in the United States today. On American television broadcasts, medical reporters regularly provide detailed descriptions of surgical procedures, complete with diagrams and anatomical drawings. Newspaper readers will find similar accounts of medical techniques ranging from heart-bypass to liposuction, from appendectomy to breast implants. Even the sports pages offer detailed explanations of how a star athlete's injured knee will be reconstructed. Many of these stories involve arcane medical facts and explore exotic surgical possibilities. The process of abortion, a commonplace occurrence, is never discussed.

Even the legal status of abortion, the topic of so many heated political debates, is ill understood today. The intense media coverage of this issue has not educated the populace. Quite the contrary; as media coverage has increased — especially in the wake of the 1989 *Webster* decision — the distortion of public opinion has become more evident. The more journalists report on abortion, the more misconceptions the American people hold.

Every year since 1965, the National Opinion Research Center has polled on the same question: "Do you think abortions should be legal under any circumstances, legal only under certain circumstances, or illegal in all circumstances." The answer have been remarkably consistent. Invariably, the "always legal" response is between 20 and 25%; "always illegal" between 17 and 21%; "legal under certain circumstances" between 52 and 59%. Although the legal status of abortion has changed dramatically over the years — most notably through the 1973 *Roe* and *Doe* decisions, and more recently through the 1989 Webster case — there are few signs of change in basic public attitudes.

However, because reporters have generally approached the issue from the perspective of women who face an unplanned pregnancy, the American public has become steadily more convinced that woman should have the right to choose abortion. Recent poll data suggest that a clear majority of Americans favor this "right to choose." According to a *Boston Globe* poll published in March 1989, solid majorities believed that abortion should be legal: to save the life of the mother (86%), in cases of rape (86%), in cases of incest (83%), if the mother's health is endangered (81%), and in cases of genetic deformity (63%).

On the other hand, while they favor the "right to choose," Americans also overwhelming favor the "right to life." The results of public-opinion polls turn on how the questions are worded. In that same *Boston Globe* survey, large majorities thought abortion should be illegal: as a means of selecting the child's sex (93%), as a means of birth control (89%), when the father is unwilling to help (83%), when the timing of the pregnancy is inconvenient (82%), when the father is absent (81%), when the woman cannot afford a child (75%), when the father pressures the mother into abortion (75%), when the father wants to keep the baby (72%), or when the pregnancy would cause emotional strain (61%).

The media focus steadily on the so-called "hard cases": pregnancies involving rape, incest, or threats to the health of the mother. But those "hard cases" account for only a minute fraction of the abortion business. According to statistics compiled by the Alan Guttmacher Institute — an affiliate of Planned Parenthood — less than five percent of all abortions are prompted by these "hard case" circumstances. The overwhelming majority of abortions are motivated by financial considerations, by problems in the parents' relationships, or by the mother's desire to postpone pregnancy. These, of course, are precisely the reasons which the American public rejects as justification for abortion. So the overwhelming majority of Americans oppose abortion in the overwhelming majority of cases.

On the eve of the *Webster* decision, a CBS News poll gave respondents a simpler choice, asking whether they would support a law banning abortion in their state except in cases of rape, incest, and the life of the mother. Such a law would be more restrictive than the laws in force in any one of the fifty states today. Yet a solid majority — sixty-six percent — said they would approve such a law.

In 1991, a Gallup poll questioned 2,100 American adults on abortion, in the largest in-depth survey ever conducted on this issue. The results confirm all previous data on American public opinion. The poll results, released in February 1991, confirm that the overwhelming majority of Americans disapprove of abortion in most circumstances and favor efforts to restrict the practice. Specifically: 91% oppose abortion as a means of selecting a baby's sex; 66% oppose abortions motivated by financial reasons; 76% oppose abortions motivated by the woman's desire to remain in school; 66% oppose abortions motivated by the woman's fear of disrupting her career; and 88% oppose using abortion as a means of birth control. Three-quarters of those surveyed believe that abortion involves deliberately taking a human life. (A 1989 *New York Times* poll found that 79% hold that belief.) Roughly half — 52% of the women polled, and 48% of the men — believe that the baby's "right to be born" should outweigh the mother's "right to choose." And despite the popular perception that abortion rights constitute a women's issue, the women polled were much more likely (by a margin of 42 to 32%) to see no moral distinction between abortion and the killing of an infant after birth.

The Gallup poll concluded that 86% of the American public support restrictions on abortion. There is especially strong public support for regulations that would give parents a voice in their daughters' decisions on abortion. Five out of six Americans polled (83%) believe that a teenage girl should consult her parents before obtaining an abortion, and 69% favor laws that would require parental consent in such cases.

Unfortunately, most Americans do not recognize the broad gap between the laws they would support and the laws in force today. Side by side with the very clear evidence of support for some legal restrictions on abortion, the Gallup poll found a shocking lack of understanding about current status American law. Nearly half of the respondents (42%) mistakenly believed that *Roe* allowed abortion only during the first three months of pregnancy, and 16% thought abortion was legal during that first trimester only if the mother's health was jeopardized. Only 10% of the American public realize that the *Roe* and *Doe* decisions make abortion legally possible throughout pregnancy, and allow unrestricted access to abortion on demand during the early stages of pregnancy.

Ever since the *Roe* and *Doe* decisions, the American pro-life movement has sought to restrict the practice of abortion. Since the public overwhelmingly backs some restrictions, pro-life activists should be able to expect public sympathy. But before that sympathy can be aroused, the American public must realize that in America today abortion is virtually unrestricted. That is a simple question of fact, easily conveyed in objective reports. But those reports have not been forthcoming; those facts have not been conveyed.

Since they mistakenly believe that abortion is already restricted, many Americans fall into a second mistake: believing that pro-life leaders are making unreasonable demands. They do not know (because the mass media do not tell them) that many pro-life initiatives involve only modest restrictions, which would win overwhelming majority support — restrictions such as parental-consent laws, or laws preventing the use of abortion as a means of sex selection. Due to the same absence of accurate reporting, the American public also remains unaware that "pro-choice" leaders adamantly oppose any such legal restrictions.

The single most compelling proof of distorted public opinion in the Gallup survey lies in the fact that 54% of the respondents characterized pro-life advocates as "extremists" and only 39% described them as belonging in the nation's political mainstream. By contrast nearly half — 48% — of those surveyed characterized pro-choice activists as members of the American mainstream. The irony is palpable. Although they embrace the same views as most pro-lifers, the majority of Americans consider those pro-lifers to be extremists.

If the media depict all pro-lifers as extremists, naturally Operation Rescue should expect particularly rough treatment. But once again, journalists do not ordinarily show their disdain openly, by slanting their stories about Rescue operations. Instead they ignore the movement; there are no stories to slant!

Since its origin in 1988, OR has staged literally hundreds of blockades at abortion clinics all over the United States. Altogether, more than fifty thousand arrests have been made — a record for civil disobedience nearly six times the total of the 1960s civil-rights movement. How many books have been written about the civil-rights movement? How many newspapers have commissioned reflective articles on that political phenomenon? How many television stations have produced special reports? The anti-war movement of the later 1960s still rates an occasional op-ed piece even today, twenty years after the fact. But very few Americans have been brought into contact with the Rescue movement. With the single exception of Randall Terry, no OR activist has become a familiar figure in the media.

Ordinarily, any movement which could mobilize several hundred people to endure arrest in the nation's capital — as OR did in November 1989 and again in November 1990 — could expect massive publicity. Photographers would chronicle the event; inquisitive reporters would want to understand — and pass along in print —the motivations behind that unusual strategy; talk-show hosts would seek out the ringleaders for prime-time appearances. OR reaped no such publicity; the "D.C. Project" went virtually unreported even by the media in Washington itself.

Or take August 1990, when leaders of the Western industrial nations gathered for an "economic summit" meeting in Houston. Journalists descended on Houston in battalion force, pouring out stories on every aspect of that city's life: the weather, the real-estate market, the fashions, the hot chili emporiums. But despite that saturation coverage, the press failed to notice that OR activists had successfully closed down abortuaries all over the city during that week.

In Wichita, of course, the Operation Rescue story became too big to ignore. But even there, the hometown *Wichita Eagle* did not deem OR worthy of front-page coverage until July 22, a whole week after the massive "Summer of Mercy" campaign began; a thousand people had blocked abortion clinics, and the Wichita Plaza had filled a hundred rooms, before the *Eagle* would admit that this was a top headline news story. The definitive *New York Times* held off front-page treatment until the number of arrests had climbed past one thousand.

Throughout that memorable Wichita summer, media coverage was spotty at best. Journalists repeatedly mentioned the death threats against Judge Kelly; they did not report the threats which Randall Terry has received; in fact, they apparently did not even think to ask Terry whether he has received death threats. (He has.) For several weeks a woman named Peggy Jarman had served as spokeswoman for Dr. Tiller's abortion clinic; then at the end of July she began identifying herself with a new group called the Pro-Choice Action League — with offices conveniently located just two doors down the street from Tiller's clinic. The national media continued quoting her extensively without bothering to mention her affiliation with Tiller. In a display of bias bordering on comedy, one reporter scolded Larry Webber, the manager of the Wichita Plaza Hotel, for his "unbusinesslike" decision to offer special rates for OR guests. While defending that decision on pure business grounds — his hotel made money on the deal — Webber also questioned his critic's business sense; the reporter qualified for that same $25 rate, yet was paying $75 a night at another hotel.

Instead of exploring the fascinating human-interest stories that OR provides, and concentrating on why so many law-abiding citizens have turned to civil disobedience, media accounts of OR have dwelt on complaints that OR uses violent or intimidating tactics. In a tense and emotional sidewalk setting, in which OR activists are invariably confronted by aggressive counter-demonstrators, such charges and countercharges are inevitable. A bodily blockade naturally involves some jostling and shoving. And since pro-abortion activists constantly complain of intimidation, journalists have every right to raise the issue. To provide a balanced treatment, however, reporters should mention that OR activists pledge to avoid all violence, "in word and in deed." And if they question the behavior of OR activists, they should hold pro-abortion demonstrators to the same standards.

Who are the counter-demonstrators? In closing one interview, a reporter asked Bill Cotter of OR-Boston whether he had missed any prominent aspect of the story. Without hesitating, Cotter shot back his answer: "The character of the opposition." At a typical Rescue site one can encounter tweedy, respectable citizens carrying attractive blue Planned-Parenthood signs, and articulate feminists with a knack for media appearances. These are the people who appear on the nightly news to denounce Operation Rescue. But one can also find militant lesbians and homosexuals, waving coathangers and condoms, carrying obscene hand-painted posters, and chanting blasphemous slogans. Those fringe characters rarely find their way onto the television newscasts, even if they dominate the scene outside the abortuary.

"In Burlington, Vermont," writes Randall Terry, "many of the supporters of Vermont Women's Health Center are avowed witches. These female sorcerers have arrived at rescues in cultic dress, beating drums, blaspheming Jesus, and crying out strange words and incantations, apparently trying to conjure up demons." In Boston, an obscure Trotskyite group arrived at one rescue, carrying an enormous, colorful banner announcing the Revolutionary Socialist Party, which they maneuvered constantly into the line of every available television camera. Somehow that banner never appeared on the night's broadcasts.

While they overlook the excesses of the pro-abortion side, journalists are quick to credit stories about pro-life misconduct. In one particularly blatant example of distortion, *Boston Globe* columnist Bella English freely expressed the opinion that Rescue activists had assaulted bystanders. Relying for evidence solely on the word of an anonymous pro-abortion counter-demonstrator — whom she identified only as "Mary" — English stated as fact that a Rescue activist had thrown himself at this defenseless woman. Only gradually did the story emerge that police on the scene had arrested "Mary" — not the Rescue activist — on assault charges, apparently for kicking the man repeatedly in the head. Even on the basis of the Bella English column, a reader would have to conclude that the Rescue activist attacked "Mary" by throwing his face at her feet — certainly an unusual form of physical assault.

When pro-lifers do take violent action, the media outrage is palpable. In 1991, pro-life militants entered an abortion clinic in suburban Chicago, where Dr. Aleksander Jakubowski conducted a practice specializing in late-term abortions, and damaged some equipment. *The New York Times* headline read: "Vandals Destroy Equipment in Illinois Gynecological Office." Notice that the motivation for that "vandalism" is not explained; the headline suggest a senseless rampage. And a "gynecological office" suggests a much more innocuous site than an abortuary. In fact, the headline is simply misleading. If the incident had been an act of random violence, it would not merit a story in an out-of-town newspaper. The *Times* printed the story only because it involved abortion, yet the headline did not mention abortion!

If they eschew violence, then, can pro-lifers expect more balanced treatment? Alas, no. Randall Terry cites the Associated Press story of his trial in Los Angeles: "Randall Terry and four of his followers in the militant anti-abortion group were acquitted of all charges stemming from an illegal demonstration." Since the jury found him innocent of criminal charges, Terry wonders, why did the AP story speak of an "illegal" demonstration?

With its predictable timing, its dramatic street tactics, and the guarantee of an emotional confrontation, Operation Rescue offers tremendous opportunities for live television coverage. A substantial live report would not only illustrate the tensions that surround the abortion debate; it would also give viewers a realistic sense of what *really happens* during these events. (The McNeil-Lehrer report provided extensive video coverage of a January 1990 rescue in Manhattan, producing some memorable footage.) Instead, television news reports have typically shown only snippets of taped reports from the scene of the action.

The lack of live coverage is especially odd, since blockades are routinely recorded on videotape by several different photographers. Local police, abortion-clinic personnel, and OR participants all bring video cameras to the events. Television camera crews do sometimes attend, adding a professional touch. There is no shortage of videotape available; in the history of the United States, no movement has ever left such a complete electronic record.

If indeed the Rescue movement is characterized by violence, surely some examples of that violent behavior should have been captured on videotape. No such examples have emerged. During the dramatic climax of the Wichita "Summer of Mercy" campaign, journalists announced grave new charges: an OR activist had assailed an abortion-clinic worker. On August 26, a Christian Broadcasting Network telecast provided video footage of the incident. The CBN clearly showed a woman in a white nurse's smock advancing belligerently toward the pro-life demonstrator, swinging at him, grabbing his camera, and pushing him backward; the pictures totally discredited the story.

So the record remains intact. Despite all the protests of OR violence, no one can produce videotaped evidence. This is a classic example of the kind of evidence Sherlock Holmes once cited: the dog that did not bark.

On the other hand, violence *against* Operation Rescue *has* been captured on videotape several times. But that is a story for another day, or at least another chapter.

8

Open Season on Pro-Lifers

WHICH SINGLE individual did the most to advance the civil-rights movement of the 1960s? Most Americans would probably name Rev. Martin Luther King, Jr. But President John F. Kennedy went to his death with a different opinion. The man who had done the most for the cause of civil rights, he told associates, was Bull Connor.

Bull Connor (for those who forget, and those too young to remember) was the commissioner of public safety for the City of Birmingham, Alabama, during the early 1960s. On his orders, Martin Luther King was arrested for leading a protest march there on Good Friday, April 12, 1963. It was Connor who encouraged the Birmingham police to loose their attack dogs on peaceful demonstrators, and to knock them down with fire hoses.

Without Bull Connor, who knows how long it might have taken the civil-rights activists to challenge the conscience of our nation? If Dr. King had not spent that Easter Sunday in prison, who knows when he might have written his classic defense of nonviolent civil disobedience, the powerful "Letter from Birmingham Jail"? Without those shocking photographs of dogs attacking demonstrators, how many Americans would have remained convinced that the Birmingham police were just doing their job — coping with people who were, after all, violating the law?

Thanks to Bull Connor, the American public suddenly confronted an ugly fact about home-style Southern justice. Whatever anyone felt about the wisdom of Martin Luther King, the violence of the police behavior was unconscionable. That violence, dramatically underscored by the nonresistance of the protesters — forced Americans to reexamine their pat assumptions about the civil-rights movement. Who really were the "good guys" in this conflict? On May 4, 1963, both *The New York Times* and *The Washington Post* gave prominent front-page treatment to the same shocking photograph, which captured a police dog — leashed but not muzzled

— lunging and snapping at a frightened Black demonstrator. The impact of that image is difficult to exaggerate. One historian (Arthur Waskow) has argued that the shock generated by that one photograph guaranteed the success of the Birmingham campaign, and even the passage of the Civil Rights Act later that year.

In 1989, pro-life activists uncovered their own equivalent of Bull Connor. But unlike their predecessors of a generation earlier, Operation Rescue activists did not receive the sympathetic attention of the nation's press. The police brutality they encountered went largely unnoticed and unrestrained.

On June 17, 1989, Rescuers from around New England converged on the quiet suburban town of West Hartford, Connecticut. Several hundred people blocked the entrance to an abortion clinic. Local police had a bit of experience with this phenomenon; a much smaller Rescue had taken place in West Hartford several weeks earlier. This time, Police Chief Robert McCue was ready.

Before they advanced on the Rescuers, the West Hartford police stopped and removed their badges. After the fact, police spokesmen said they took this action to avoid scratching themselves or the people they arrested — a claim that sounds absurd in the light of what was about to happen. Rescuers counter that the police removed their badges so that victims of brutality could not easily identify their assailants.

Then the police began to remove the Rescuers. But Rescuers were not the only people arrested. Three journalists — Sheila Chase of *The Staten Island Advance*, Dale O'Leary of Boston's *The Pilot*, and Inez Casademont, a Boston television producer — were among the first people arrested. All three women had legitimate press credentials, and none was participating in the blockade. But the police took them into custody; in fact the journalists were among the first people the police removed from the scene. Notes, film, and videotape were destroyed. Only snatches of videotape footage would emerge to document the West Hartford Rescue.

With those inquisitive members of the press out of the way, the police waded into the unresisting Rescuers with an astonishing show of physical force. Knees, elbows, fists, and billy clubs flew in every direction. The violence was as indiscriminate as it was intense.

Lillian Loughlin, a grandmother, had come to the clinic as a prayer supporter, not intending to risk arrest and not participating in the blockade. But as she stood in the parking lot, she was suddenly knocked down from behind by a police officer. When her husband rushed to intervene, he too was wrestled face-down to the ground. "I never believed it when blacks and protestors yelled police brutality," Mrs. Laughlin later told Nat Hentoff of *The Village Voice*; "Now, I'm inclined to listen." Linda Thayer, a schoolteacher in Boston's inner city, told Hentoff: "I tell you that I feel safer there among the druglords than I did that day in June among the police of West Hartford."

When the dust settled, 261 Rescuers had been arrested. Of these, 31 suffered broken bones, dislocated joints, or eye injuries that required medical attention. One priest was beaten so badly that friends did not recognize him. A woman who reported to a local hospital for treatment was asked whether she had been involved in a motorcycle accident.

With the Rescuers in custody, the official misconduct continued. Police knelt on Rescuers' wrists while applying handcuffs, then with the cuffs in place, and both arms pinned behind their backs, the police slipped a club between the Rescuers' arms and lifted them — putting enormous strain and pain on the arms and shoulders. John Leo of *U.S. News and World Report* saw the attitude of the police department exhibited on the department's own videotape: "At one point an arrested man asks, 'Who is the arresting officer?' And Chief McCue responds, 'One of them is the guy with his knee on your chin'" When one West Hartford resident filed a formal complaint, a police detective soon appeared on his doorstep — not to investigate his complaint but to probe his own involvement in the pro-life movement.

Nat Hentoff, writing a series of articles about West Hartford for *The Village Voice*, looked for a plausible explanation of the police violence. He found his man. Lt. Patrick Allard, a police-academy instructor, had given the West Hartford force some tips on controlling demonstrations. "You must maintain tactical alertness," Allard warned: "Compassion is a human quality that interferes with tactical alertness." He heartily recommends "pain compliance" holds to ensure that prisoners will obey the officers' will. In his view, anyone — no matter how passive, no matter how obviously nonviolent — is a threat to the health of the arresting officer. In police training sessions, Allard makes an implausible claim: "A passive demonstrator in front of an abortion clinic is as risky as a person coming out of a bank with a gun."

Since they went into the confrontation with that no-holds-barred attitude, it is not surprising that the West Hartford police made no apologies for their behavior. Chief McCue announced, "I commend every single member of my team." The West Hartford town council adopted a resolution congratulating the police for their "professional and sensitive handling" of the Rescue. And *The Hartford Courant*, in a news story, deflected all criticism back onto Operation Rescue: "By itself, the protestors' choice of West Hartford over more hospitable towns raises the question of whether they wanted a police confrontation. Their subsequent use of the brutality charges to whip up support for their cause makes that question all the more pertinent."

Even after the trauma of their arrest, the West Hartford defendants had not seen the end of the official misconduct. John Leo of *U.S. News* reports: "Some of those arrested were not allowed a single phone call for as long as five days. When permitted, these calls were monitored by authorities, which is unconstitutional." Finally, badly bruised and shaken by their experience, the Rescuers were hauled into court — sometimes literally. Again Leo tells the story: "When they were finally arraigned on the third day, the courtroom was closed the public, and police were allowed to use pain holds on prisoners right in front of the judge, though one judge sharply forbade it."

With the honorable exceptions of Nat Hentoff and John Leo, the violence of West Hartford was virtually ignored by journalists outside the pro-life movement. Sheila Chase of *The Staten Island Advance* did write a story about her experience in prison, bitterly protesting the gross violation of her First-Amendment rights. But even that cause — which normally mobilizes the press instantly — failed to move the major media. When John Spear of the *Orange County Post* attacked the brutality of the West Hartford police in a memorable editorial entitled "Northern Rednecks," the town fathers of West Hartford slapped him with a federal lawsuit. Again the episode raised obvious First-Amendment questions, yet again the other members of the press remained silent. Dozens of vivid photographs of the West Hartford incident did survive the police efforts and became readily available to anyone interested in the topic. But those photographs did not appear on the front page of *The New York Times* — or any other page. The *Times* printed just one story on the West Hartford arrests: a report about crowded conditions in Connecticut jails.

West Hartford was by no means the only instance of police brutality against Operation Rescue. From the earliest days of the Rescue movement, some police departments have seen violence as an efficient method of discouraging pro-life activism. In 1988, when the continuing siege of Atlanta began to wear down the patience of law-enforcement officials, OR leaders held a meeting with Atlanta police officials. Joseph Foreman reports being told: "We're tired of you, of treating you with kid gloves; we're going to be taking them off." Immediately thereafter, in October 1988, Rescuers saw a tremendous increase in the use of physical force, and Atlanta's finest began the commonplace use of "pain compliance" holds.

When police officers use "pain compliance" techniques — twisting back the arms of the people they are arresting, or hooking a thumb under the jawbone, or bending fingers backward to the wrist, or pressing on nerve centers in the neck, or shoving their own fingers up the person's nostrils — they can cause excruciating pain, and usually "persuade" the subject to follow their orders quickly. A Rescuer whose wrist is bent in a "come-along" hold might well begin to walk under his own power, rather than forcing the police to carry him away from the clinic. So "pain compliance" does help clear the clinic doors more speedily. At the same time, the tactics usually convince other would-be Rescuers, who see or hear about the pain their friends have endured, that they should not risk the same treatment. Pain is a great motivator and a great deterrent.

However, the deliberate use of pain as a crowd-control tactic raises serious ethical questions. When the police in Third World countries use "pain compliance" on dissidents, human-rights advocates call it torture. When Atlanta police began to use these tactics, they were roundly denounced by Hosea Williams, a veteran of the civil-rights campaign who had marched with Martin Luther

King in Selma and Birmingham. But most civil libertarians looked the other way, and the campaign of intimidation continued.

Physical violence was not the only technique used to discourage pro-life activism. Religious rights were also threatened. In Atlanta, Rev. Norman Weslin, a Catholic priest, was put in solitary confinement for the "offense" of saying a Mass in jail while imprisoned for Rescue activities. Sexual harassment occurred as well — often barely distinguishable from pain-control tactics. In Buffalo, New York, Erie County Sheriff Thomas Higgins admitted that one officer "did, indeed, grab several male protestors by the genitals to get them to cooperate in fingerprinting and booking procedures."

The most appalling outburst of sexual abuse of Rescuers occurred in Pittsburgh in March 1989. Sixty female Rescuers detained in the Allegheny County jail reported that they had been subjected to sexual threats and innuendo; others say that guards fondled their breasts and genitals. Several women had their blouses and sweaters pulled up over their heads. One woman was dragged in front of male prisoners with her breasts fully exposed; another had her pants pulled down. (Warden Charles Kozakiewicz, who was responsible for the care of women in the prison facility, had already lost one prior lawsuit on brutality charges.)

The prospect of a term in jail is never pleasant, but Rescue veterans began to recognize the implicit threat that made prison so much more frightening. "When you listen to cops and judges, you begin to see that in their minds, the real deterrent built into the American judicial system is the threat of homosexual rape," writes Joan Andrews. "That threat is never made official, but it is the real core of the prison society in this once-civilized nation."

On at least one occasion, the threat was not at all subtle. When Rescuers annoyed prison officials in Cranston, Rhode Island, by refusing to reveal their Social Security numbers, one rescuer reports that a prison official told him he might change his mind "once you have a boyfriend." That rescuer was then put into an isolated cell, along with several hardened criminals who proceeded with similar threats. When they actually laid hands on him, the Rescuer called for prison guards and promised to provide his Social Security number. Outraged, Operation Rescue called a press conference to denounced the sexual harassment. But the New England media generally refused o air the charges, explaining that they could not be proven. This occurred in November 1991 — just a few weeks after the American media had given two full weeks of headline coverage to the unsubstantiated charges of sexual harassment leveled by Anita Hill against Supreme Court nominee Clarence Thomas.

Milder forms of abuse are commonplace in prisons. Rescuers have been placed in cells that are overheated or unheated, depending on the season. They can be deprived of necessary medicine. Their meals can be delayed. They can be overcrowded. On New Year's Day of 1989, sixteen men were crammed into a jail cell in Brookline, Massachusetts, that had been designed to accommodate just two people. Their attorney, Neil Sullivan, compared the conditions unfavorably to the Black Hole of Calcutta.

More ordinary forms of "pain compliance" were used during the 'Holy Week Rescues" in Los Angeles in March 1989. Police officials bent and twisted arms and fingers; they thrust knuckles under jawbones, noses, and eye sockets. Debbie Grumbine, the mother of eight children, did not realize that she was five weeks pregnant when she risked arrest; she subsequently suffered a miscarriage which her doctor attributed to traumatic nerve damage.

Los Angeles also provided the Rescue movement with its most stunning and compelling evidence of police brutality. Unlike their colleagues in West Hartford, the Los Angeles police did not confiscate videotape. So there is abundant footage, readily available to anyone who wants it, of the police violence. Using nunchakas, an Oriental martial-arts weapon that is ordinarily illegal in California, the police inflicted frightening pain on one unresisting Rescuer after another in June 1988. The resulting agony is eloquently conveyed by the contorted faces of the Rescuers. And in one particularly sickening episode the police bend back Michael Housman's arm a bit too far, and it breaks. The ugly sound of the snapping bone is clearly audible on the videotape; the crazy angle at which Shorter's arm dangles offers graphic, enduring proof of the brutality.

Rescuers lodge complaints, of course, when they are victimized by police misconduct. But to date those complaints have prompted only the most minimal bureaucratic response. In Boston, the septuagenarian Dr. Joseph Stanton, deprived of the canes he needs to walk, was dragged into a police station and tossed headlong into an elevator by one policeman, who compounded the insult by spouting a stream of obscenities; then two other Rescuers were thrown on top of Stanton's prone body. Dr. Stanton suffered two broken ribs, and a friend, former Boston Mayor John Collins, lodged a protest with federal and local government authorities. U.S. Attorney Wayne Budd promised an investigation, and the F.B.I. was assigned to interview witnesses. One year later, the F.B.I. had not even interviewed Dr. Stanton himself.

A similar fate awaited the women who entered charges of sexual harassment after their nightmarish stay in Allegheny County jail. After months of official inaction, the women brought their complaints to Washington. Finally four members of Congress — Reps. Robert Dornan, Bob Walker, Christ Smith, and Clyde Holloway — wrote to the federal prosecutor, complaining that the F.B.I. office assigned to investigate the Pittsburgh incidents "was more interested in those participating in Operation Rescue than in [the women's] mistreatment at the jail." After months of constant nagging from pro-life supporters and bland demurrals from federal investigators, the Justice Department issued a routine statement early in 1991, announcing that the evidence of brutality against OR was inconclusive, and the investigation ended. Don Feder asked a pointed question in his *Boston Herald* column, "Does a night stick breaking the bones of a pro-life protestor make a sound? Apparently not, if no one in the Justice Department hears it."

William Allen, the chairman of the U.S. Civil Rights Commission, felt his own level of frustration mounting as he saw law-enforcement officials ignoring the evidence of brutality. Although he did not share the convictions of the pro-life leaders, Allen did take his commission's mandate seriously, and he called for hearings on the issue. But then, Allen told *The Wall Street Journal*, he received a thinly veiled threat from the congressman who controlled his funding. Rep. Don Edwards, who chaired the Judiciary Committee group charged with oversight for the Civil Rights Commission, warned Allen that an investigation of OR-related police violence "appears to violate the commission's authorizing statute" which forbids work on abortion, and could "seriously erode congressional confidence" in the group. Despite the chairman's protests, the full commission refused to schedule hearings. Soon

Allen was deposed as chairman, and once again the public discussion of police violence against pro-lifers quietly died.

What would it take to bring about that discussion? Randall Terry expressed his exasperation in an interview with *Time* magazine: "What has irritated me most is that if we were any other group that was politically correct there would be a hue and cry from the media and the civil rights groups over such tactics. But because we are pro-lifers, because we are not a currently hip cause, we are ignored."

In Washington, D.C., liberal political activists mobilized their forces during 1984 to stage daily picketing outside the South African embassy, calling attention to human-rights complaints against that country. Each day, prominent public figures (including, among others, the city's mayor) would arrive on the scene, and the police would politely take them into custody — pausing in the act just long enough for the ever-present news photographers to take their obligatory shots. The entire event was carefully choreographed and painstakingly polite. Those arrested were released within an hour. There was never a hint of confrontation, nor a whiff of official misconduct. Yet that staged controversy received media coverage all across the country. Protests against South Africa were as popular in 1984 as pro-life blockades are unpopular in 1990. Terry had a point.

Armando Valladares, the U.S. Ambassador to the United Nations Commission on Human Rights, has impeccable credentials to speak out against police brutality. He knows the consequences of official misconduct first-hand, having spent twenty-three years as a prisoner in Fidel Castro's Cuban jails. The October 1991 issue of *New Dimensions* magazine carried his long, forceful statement on the charges surrounding Operation Rescue:

> "There have been allegations of police brutality against people who were peacefully trying to rescue babies from abortion by blockading the entrances to abortion clinics in various cities in the United States. These allegations are backed by sworn affidavits from victims and eyewitnesses, and, in many cases, photographic and videotaped evidence which I myself have seen. It is important to recognize that these brutal acts are completely unwarranted and unnecessary, and that they seem to be designed 'to teach people a lesson.'

"Rescuers are acting to protect the rights of unborn babies, and do not believe that in doing so they are violating any law. But even if they are, they are doing so in a completely peaceful and nonviolent manner. They merely sit (or kneel) and pray or sing religious hymns. They even pray for the police officers who arrest and/or abuse them.

"Yet in many cases, 'pain compliance' was inflicted on rescuers even after they had been removed from the site, had agreed to leave the site, or were unable to leave because they were pinned to the pavement by police officers. In one instance, 900 peaceful citizens were subjected to such punitive violence.

"It should be duly noted that many police departments do not even arrest rescuers. Most departments handle them gently and respectfully in making arrests. The alleged 'crime' committed by rescuers is a misdemeanor for which police are not required to make arrests.

"These attacks are reminiscent of those made against an earlier generation, another nonviolent civil rights movement, under similar circumstances during the 1960s. At that time, 6,000 citizens were arrested and the President and Attorney General were forced to take decisive action to ensure that the federal government brought police brutality and the official complicity therein to a halt. Similar action is needed today."

The American people set high standards for police behavior and view charges of police brutality quite seriously. A *New York Times* poll (published April 5, 1991) revealed that sixty-seven percent of respondents are "likely to think the charges are justified" when they hear complaints about police brutality. The prospect of negative publicity, and the attendant official scrutiny, is a primary deterrent against police misconduct. But if the public at large does not hear the complaints, or see the available evidence of police violence, over-aggressive police officers can continue to operate with impunity. For years, the sad record of official violence against Black people remained outside the consciousness of ordinary Americans. The dramatic confrontations in Alabama early in the 1960s — the images of Bull Connor's water cannon and attack dogs — marked a watershed point in the civil-rights movement. Once the American public saw unmistakable evidence of police misconduct, the Black activists received markedly better civil-rights protection.

In some cases, OR's complaints have produced the same results. From Los Angeles, Susan Finn of OR told the *National Catholic Register* that by 1991 police were only making arrests in roughly fifty percent of Rescue incidents, and the arrests were not nearly as violent as they were during those horrible days of the Holy Week Rescues. Nunchakas had been abandoned, and the police were "treating us like a credible group of people instead of a group of crazy fanatics."

Unfortunately, the turnabout in the conduct of Los Angeles police was not typical. For that matter, it could probably be explained by factors completely unrelated to Operation Rescue. In March 1991, when Los Angeles police officials severely beat an unarmed Back motorist named Rodney King, the beating was caught on a hidden videocamera. Tapes of that disgraceful incident were shown repeatedly by television news stations all around the country, and the Los Angeles police force came under heavy attack for its use of violence. In that climate, the decidedly less brutal treatment of OR activists might have reflected a simple desire to avoid inflaming the controversy.

Despite the vicious abuse of Rodney Gates, most media outlets saw no reason to reexamine old charges of police brutality against OR. After seeing tapes of the Gates beating broadcast repeatedly on local television stations, and hearing dozens of complaints about widespread brutality within the Los Angeles police force, one pro-life activist in Boston offered to give the media there a new angle on the question. He wrote to every television news station in the area, offering — free of charge — a broadcast-quality videotape of an incident from the Holy Week Rescues in which Michael Housman's arm was snapped by police nunchakas. Not a single television station even acknowledged the offer.

9

Justice Is Deaf

IMAGINE THAT you have a very unsociable next-door neighbor who has a large swimming pool in his backyard. Time after time, this crochety neighbor has informed you that you are not welcome in his yard, and that you may not use his swimming pool under any circumstances. You can take a hint; you stay away.

But then one day, while you are mowing your own lawn, you notice that a small baby is crawling unattended across your neighbor's backyard. As you watch in horror, the baby approaches the swimming pool, and tumbles in. What do you do?

Naturally, you jump over the fence, dive into the pool, and save the baby's life. If your neighbor is foolish enough to press charges for trespassing, no jury in the country will convict you. Under ordinary circumstances your actions would have constituted trespassing, but these were not ordinary circumstances. You quite justifiably discarded one good — your neighbor's property rights — to serve a much higher good — the baby's life. Your action was not a crime but a display of admirable quick thinking, possibly even heroism. At your trial (if the case went that far) your attorney would wrap up all these arguments by invoking an age-old principle of Anglo-American law: the necessity defense.

Recognized in common-law practice for centuries, the necessity defense is enshrined (in somewhat different terms, and under different names) in legal precedents and statutes throughout the United States. When radical activists led by Abbie Hoffman (and including Amy Carter, the president's daughter) staged a sit-in to disrupt CIA recruiting activities in Amherst, Massachusetts, they invoked the necessity defense successfully and avoided punishment for their demonstration. But despite that precedent, judges in Massachusetts have refused to allow Rescuers to use the necessity defense in their trials. And that unhappy pattern has been duplicated all across the country.

If a jury hears the necessity defense — that is, if the presiding judge allows defense lawyers to introduce that argument in court — then the defense may win its case. Even if the trial judge does not allow the defense to introduce the necessity defense, Rescuers can rely on another strong argument. When the evidence clearly indicates that their actions did fulfill the standard definition of trespassing, Rescue defendants can fall back on another time-honored legal principle: jury nullification. If the members of a jury believe that a law is fundamentally unjust, or that its application in a particular case is obviously wrong-headed, then those jurors have the right to render a not-guilty verdict, even in the face of overwhelming evidence.

Even before the American Revolution, John Adams made the case for jury nullification, teaching that if a juror believes that the prosecution is advancing its cause unjustly, "It is not only his right but his duty in that case to find the verdict according to his own best understanding, judgment, and conscience, though in direct opposition to the direction of the court."

Unfortunately, most American jurors today are unfamiliar with their own legal rights and responsibilities. If the judge presiding over a Rescue trial tells jurors to ignore the defendants' motivations, the jurors usually obey. But then the case boils down to a simple question of fact — did the defendants trespass or not? — and a guilty verdict is inevitable.

On rare occasions, Rescue defendants have invoked the necessity defense successfully. In August 1989, Judge Gerhard wrote a memorable opinion exonerating St. Louis Rescuers: "This court finds that the credible evidence in these cases establishes justification for the defendants' actions. Their violations of the ordinances involved here were necessary as emergency measures to avoid the imminent private injuries of death and maiming of unborn children, which imminent deaths and maimings were occasioned through no fault of the defendants but occasioned by the operation of a lucrative commercial endeavor."

But Judge Gerhard is a rarity. Far more frequently, Rescue defendants have complained bitterly about judges who rode roughshod over their constitutional rights. The mound of OR complaints about judicial misconduct has grown just as steadily as the Rescue movement itself, and each new landmark in Rescue history seems to engender a new complaint.

When Joan Andrews was arrested in Pensacola in March 1986, the judge who presided over her bail hearing stipulated that if she was involved in another "incident" at the same abortion mill, her bail would be revoked. But the judge specifically refused to grant one crucial request by the abortionists' lawyer, which would have prohibited Joan and her fellow defendants from coming near the clinic. Joan felt that distinction was clear, as she reports: "To me — and to any intelligent human being — 'incident' meant something like creating a ruckus or doing something that incurs an arrest. So we did not worry about going back to picket the place." So with two friends, Joan quietly picketed the Pensacola abortuary for a few hours. To her astonishment, the judge revoked her bail.

When Operation Rescue reached a new high-water mark in Atlanta during the summer of 1988, Michael McMonagle came to trial on charges of aiding and abetting the blockade of an abortion clinic. McMonagle claimed that at the time in question he was not involved in the blockade; he was standing across the street from the abortuary, exhorting the police to be gentle. McMonagle's defense offered to introduce a videotape which clearly showed that he was on the opposite side of the street. The trial judge would not allow the jury to see the tape.

In March 1989, the "Holy Week Rescues" brought still more thousands of pro-life activists onto the streets of Los Angeles, and authorities looked for a new way to send a strong message. Most of the Rescuers were charged with simple trespass. But when Randall Terry was arrested, officials threw the book at him. As he explains in *Accessory to Murder*, "The authorities charged me and three others with felony conspiracies to commit misdemeanor trespass. Absurd, isn't it?"

Terry eventually beat the charge in Los Angeles, but Andrews and McMonagle were both found guilty. Joan Andrews was sentenced to five years in prison. Michael McMonagle was originally assessed a forty-five-day sentence and a thousand dollars fine, but when he refused to pay the fine, Judge Thelma Cummings increased his sentence to six months. For his role in the Atlanta Rescues, Randall Terry was hit with a two-year suspended sentence and a thousand dollars fine. He too refused to pay the fine, so Judge John Brunner extended his sentence to two years. Terry served four months in a Georgia prison camp before an anonymous donor paid his fine and obtained his release.

"Compared to the sentences of other protest groups in Atlanta our sentences have been outrageous," Terry points out. "An anti-Ku Klux Klan group gathered in Atlanta during the Democratic National Convention to protest the Ku Klux Klan. They threw bricks, some of which hurt the police. They were all fined one hundred dollars. A group of anti-nuclear protestors were also arrested during the convention. They served three days in jail, had a twenty-five-dollar fine suspended, and went home. When disabled veterans sat in at the federal building in Atlanta (coincidentally, during the week of my trial), President Bush himself called and asked that they not be arrested! Homosexuals lay down in the streets and were fined seventy dollars and released."

Those stiff sentences handed out in the Georgia courtrooms came after the Atlanta City Council won a court injunction against Operation Rescue. The injunction imposed strict limits on demonstrations and picketing near abortion clinics: no more than twenty people could come within fifty feet of the abortuaries; no Rescuer could come within five feet of people entering the clinic. Although that injunction stirred a hornet's nest of constitutional issues — it constituted a prior restraint on political protest, inhibited the free speech of sidewalk counselors, and limited the Rescuers' rights to free assembly — the Georgia Supreme Court upheld it, citing the government's "significant interest in the right of citizens to obtain desired medical service." The U.S. Supreme Court refused to consider a Rescue appeal.

When Operation Rescue came to New York, pro-abortion leaders had learned their lessons from the Atlanta case. The National Organization for Women (NOW) sought a federal injunction against the Rescues, basing their case on an obscure nineteenth-century statute that had been enacted after the Civil War to protect the newly emancipated slaves from harassment by the Ku Klux Klan. Just as the Klan singled out Black citizens for abuse, NOW told the court, Operation Rescue singles out women. Remarkably, the court accepted that argument. And the Second Circuit Court of Appeal rejected OR's appeal in *NOW v. Terry*, finding that "defendants engaged in a conspiracy to prevent women from obtaining access to

119

medical facilities" and that since the "conspiracy is focused entirely on women seeking abortions, their actions reveal an attitude or animus based on gender."

Could a movement such as OR, in which thousands of women are active participants, be reasonably classified as a conspiracy against women? Evidently the U.S. Supreme Court thought so; the high court again refused to hear an OR appeal in *NOW v. Terry*.

Now the opponents of OR had a powerful legal weapon in their hands, and a powerful legal precedent to cite. Federal suits based on the old Ku Klux Klan Act were filed in courtrooms all across the country. Finally, in the Virginia suburbs just across the Potomac River from Washington, OR found an appropriate test case. Jayne Bray — an attractive young women active in the local Rescue network — became the leading figure in *Bray v. Alexandria*, which challenged an injunction handed down against Virginia Rescuers. In the federal district OR lost the case, as the court cited the precedents established by *NOW v. Terry* and other similar suits: "the majority of courts have concluded that a gender-based animus satisfies the conspiracy requirements." But OR again petitioned the Supreme Court, and by this time the composition of that Court had changed significantly. Justice David Souter had replaced William Brennan, and Thurgood Marshall had retired (Clarence Thomas had not yet joined the Court) when the Court finally heard oral arguments on the *Bray* case in the fall of 1991.

(Aside from furnishing the material for a Supreme Court challenge, *Bray v. Alexandria* also illustrated how abortion supporters used lawsuits as offensive weapons against Rescue leaders. Michael McMonagle and Randall Terry were both named as defendants in the lawsuit that gave rise to the *Bray* case; yet both were in prison in Atlanta at the time when the suit was filed. Patrick Mahoney rolled up twenty-six thousand dollars in legal bills on the case, although he had never been arrested in Virginia.)

By the time the Supreme Court heard the *Bray* case, the use of federal lawsuits based on the Ku Klux Klan Act had become the focus of an enormous controversy in Wichita. Judge Patrick Kelly had granted an injunction, OR had appealed, and the U.S. Justice Department had intervened on behalf of the Rescuers. The Justice Department's intervention was not unprecedented; federal attorneys had taken the same stance in the *Bray* case. But Judge Kelly's intemperate reaction thrust this rather arcane controversy onto the nation's headlines.

Rushing onto ABC's *Nightline* telecast (where correspondent Jackie Judd misinformed the audience by saying that OR had "suddenly" won the administration's support), Judge Kelly began his blast at the Attorney General by saying of the Justice Department brief that "it's not legal. There isn't any validity to it, and it is political, if for any other reason." (The Tenth Circuit Court of Appeal evidently disagreed; in October that court voided Kelly's order requiring a hundred-thousand-dollar "peace bond" for Rescue leaders. And since the Supreme Court agreed to hear the *Bray* case, evidently the nation's top judicial body agreed that the Rescuers' case had merit.) Even host Barbara Walters, who made little effort to conceal her disagreement with the Rescue position, seemed surprised by Kelly's aggressiveness, asking him whether it was not "very unusual for a federal judge sitting on a case to come out publicly as you are doing tonight." The Ku Klux Klan Act allows for civil lawsuits against anyone who conspires to deprive "any person or class of persons of the equal protection of the law." Abortionists claim that OR meets that definition — that "a conspiracy against a class of women of childbearing age, pregnant and seeking help, is a conspiracy against women."

In the Wichita case Jay Sekulow and Patrick Monaghan, lawyers for the Rescue leaders, argued in vain that the Ku Klux Klan Act was irrelevant to the case. They claimed that women seeking abortions are "not really a class at all; rather it is an activity dressed up to look like a class." Several weeks later, in a *New York Times* opinion column, their argument drew support from William Bradford Reynolds, former director of the Justice Department's civil rights division, who saw the absurdity of the charge: "The millions of Americans who advocate childbirth rather than abortion are, in Judge Kelly's court, engaged in invidious sex discrimination."

The Supreme Court decision in the *Bray* case (still pending as this book goes to press) will at least temporarily settle the question of whether Rescues can be blocked by federal courts. But ironically even Patrick Monaghan, who argued so forcefully against Judge Kelly's injunction, doubts that the *Bray* case will have a decisive impact on the legal problems confronting Operation Rescue. Although federal lawsuits generate national publicity, he points out, the federal courts can be unwieldy, and enforcement efforts can be subject to considerable political pressure. Monaghan observes, "Frankly, the places where law-enforcement authorities have handled Rescues most effectively have been the cases where local authorities have handled it. The feds do not handle these things well. The local community is more capable of handling protest movements.'"

The local community is also capable of enacting its own legislation, creating restrictions on OR far more specific and severe than those of the Ku Klux Klan Act. In New Jersey, when pro-abortion legislators introduced a bill that would have outlawed blockades and even sidewalk counseling, William Bolan of the state's Catholic Conference warned: "An attempt to dissuade a woman from allowing an abortionist to kill her unborn child will become illegal."

In states where the political leadership responds to the desires of the abortion industry, federal lawsuits are unnecessary; state courts handle the cases far more expeditiously. In Massachusetts, the state's attorney general joined abortionists in seeking an injunction against clinic blockades. Shopping around for a sympathetic judge, the plaintiffs ignored Norfolk and Suffolk Counties, where most of the state's Rescues had taken place, and brought their action before Judge Peter Lauriat in Middlesex County. They were not disappointed. Although the abortionists' case alleged that OR had deprived women of their civil "right" to an abortion, they did not produce a single witness to testify that she had been unable to procure an abortion. Nevertheless Judge Lauriat granted the injunction.

Operation Rescue-Boston defied that injunction almost immediately, with Rescues in Brookline and Boston. Three pro-life activists were soon hauled up on contempt charges for staging those blockades. Brookline is located in Norfolk County, Boston in Suffolk County; the Fourth Amendment guarantees that defendants will be tried in the jurisdiction in which their alleged crime occurred. OR lawyers asked for a trial in Norfolk County. Their motion was denied. Bill Cotter, Darroline Firlit, and Sean Brogan were soon convicted —and sentenced to terms of up to one year — in a Middlesex County court.

Did that trial in Massachusetts raise serious questions about the constitutional rights of the OR defendants? Absolutely. But it was not the first time that Rescuers had seen a judge abridge the protections guaranteed by the Bill of Rights. The Rescuers' freedom of religion and their right to an effective defense in criminal trials were frequently misplaced.

In Wichita, Judge Kelly had ordered Rev. Phil Vollman of Cleveland arrested when Rev. Vollman confronted the abortionist Dr. Tiller with the warnings found in Psalm 37: "The wicked, enemies of Yahweh, will be destroyed." Pastor Skip Robokoff was also arrested, at an abortuary in Dobbs Ferry, New York, for shouting scriptural references to divine judgment. Assistant Village Justice James Badie forbade preaching by Robokoff within a hundred yards of the sidewalks where he had been arrested.

During trials in San Diego, in October 1989, the Rescuers' attorney Cyrus Zal was ordered to refrain from any mention of abortion during his presentation. Judge Larry Brainard insisted that the trial must focus exclusively on the charges of trespassing, so he compiled a list of 21 words which Zal could not use, including fetus, abortion, murder, rescue, baby, etc. Judge Brainard also ordered Zal and his defendants to refrain from prayer — even silent prayer — in his courtroom! When he "slipped" and mentioned some of the taboo words, Zal was hit with twenty contempt citations, bringing a nine-month sentence on the lawyer himself!

Needless to say, in all of these cases the court provided legal reasoning to justify its actions. A full examination of those legal arguments would require an effort far beyond the scope of this book. But at the very least, these remarkable judicial opinions seem to impinge on the constitutional liberties that all American citizens cherish. Why did the extraordinary orders issued by these judges escape media scrutiny? Why were there no panels of legal scholars assigned to explore the ramifications of the court decisions? Ordinarily, the American Civil Liberties Union (ACLU) maintains a near-absolute insistence on the sweep of the freedoms guaranteed by the Bill of Rights. Where was the ACLU in these cases?

In Southern California, the ACLU was indeed active — on the

opposite side of the issue. In *Accessory to Murder* Randall Terry devotes an entire chapter to his indictment of the ACLU. Among his charges: "When Operation Rescue came to Los Angeles in 1989, the ACLU opposed us with unrelenting fervor. Carol Sobbells, pro-abortionist feminist and attorney for the ACLU, met with Police Chief Darryl Gates, insisting that they vigorously enforce trespass laws and that we be arrested at any rescues. The ACLU then completely betrayed its own policy — and remained faithful to child-killing — secured an injunction against rescues, and sued us."

On rare occasions the ACLU did intervene on Rescuers' behalf, but only when the question was completely divorced from the central issue of abortion. In 1991, the Rhode Island ACLU chapter prepared an *amicus* brief supporting Rescuers when a local judge ordered them to reveal their Social Security numbers. The brief was carefully written to address only the propriety of demanding that defendants release their Social Security numbers — a point on which federal law clearly sides with the Rescuers.

More typically, when Rescue cases produced knotty questions of constitutional rights, the ACLU stood aside. John Leo of *U.S. News and World Report* asked why, and answered his own question: "Why is it that the ACLU, which happily defends the Nazis and the Klan, has such trouble helping abused abortion protestors? Well, for one thing, the ACLU has an abortion lobby inside it (the Reproductive Freedom Project)." A defense of Rescue activists would pit one arm of the ACLU against another. Perhaps even more importantly, it might alienate the ACLU from its financial supporters. Leo quoted the indefatigable civil-libertarian gadfly Alan Dershowitz: "You can make more money supporting reproductive rights than you can supporting civil liberties. It's as simple as that."

No one is immune from a lawsuit, and anyone who participates in a Rescue blockade runs the risk of being singled out for legal punishment. How do pro-abortion leaders choose their victims? Understandably, their first targets are the leaders of the Rescue movement; Randall Terry has been named as defendant in cities that he has never visited. But the pro-abortion forces have other criteria in mind as well.

Chris Slattery might have seemed like an ordinary young professional, working in the advertising industry and raising his family in New York. But Slattery was unique in one respect: he ran the only crisis-pregnancy center on the island of Manhattan that operated with a pro-life mission. Due to his efforts, at least three thousand women had received counseling, clothing, housing, and advice about adoption, allowing them to avoid abortion.

Slattery had also become active in Operation Rescue. And although Judge Robert Ward had issued a temporary injunction against OR, in response to NOW's lawsuit based on the Ku Klux Klan Act, Slattery felt the call to help save unborn children. He spoke out at Rescue rallies, and in October 1988, when OR blocked a clinic in Dobbs Ferry, New York, Slattery served as the group's principal contact with the media. Throughout the Rescue he stood across the street, talking with reporters. Slattery was not named in the injunction, and he didn't participate in the blockade. It didn't matter. When his case came before the court, Judge Ward slapped Slattery with a twenty-five-thousand-dollar fine for breaking the injunction.

Long before that case came to trial, however, Slattery had taken part in another Rescue action. In January 1989, he was one of 1,800 Rescuers arrested in Manhattan, just a few days after Judge Ward announced that his injunction would apply permanently. For that offense Judge Ward added another $25,000 fine, plus attorneys' fees.

Slattery had fought hard to resist the NOW lawsuit. When process servers appeared at his home, he and his wife refused to answer the door. At work, he became accustomed to ducking out the back door of his office when an unfamiliar face appeared at the reception desk. Colleagues began asking uncomfortable questions; feminists scribbled denunciations on the walls of the ladies' restroom in his office building. Eventually Slattery lost his job, and soon he lost his financial future. Including attorneys' fees, the legal judgment assessed against him could approach two hundred thousand dollars. Even filing for personal bankruptcy would not eliminate the problem, Slattery confided to Ray Kerrison of the *New York Post*; "They can take ten percent of my salary for twenty years."

In a pair of eloquent columns pleading Slattery's case, Ray Kerrison compared Slattery's fate with the sentences doled out to homosexual activists who had blocked access to New York's state capitol building in Albany. Most of the homosexual protestors received hundred-dollar fines; a few repeat offenders were penalized with two-hundred-dollar levies.

In some contempt-of-court cases, judges impose enormous fines in an effort to force recalcitrant parties to obey the court's orders. A wayward father who does not make child-support payments, for instance, could be hit with stiff daily fines until he makes those payments, thereby purging himself of contempt. But Slattery could do nothing to purge himself; he could not undo his past actions. So why did Judge Ward assess these extreme penalties? Why had the NOW lawsuit singled him out from among the thousands of Rescue activists in New York? Slattery himself had no questions. Remember that his crisis-pregnancy center had deprived the abortion industry of customers, and his leadership in OR had enticed new recruits into the movement. "They're trying to put a chill in the hearts of committed pro-life people," he concluded.

How could a quiet, civic-minded family man like Chris Slattery become the target for a legal vendetta? Attorney Patrick Monaghan refers to "the abortion-distortion factor" which has infected so many court cases, with the result that "the law is turned topsy-turvy." Nowhere is that distortion more evident than in the use of "RICO" suits against Rescuers.

The federal Racketeer Influenced and Corrupt Organizations (RICO) Act of 1962 was originally devised to give prosecutors a new weapon against organized crime. With broad powers and stiff penalties, RICO gave federal attorneys the choice of civil or criminal prosecution, and allowed wide latitude for lawsuits based on a "conspiracy" to commit criminal activity. Because it was written to incorporate those broad powers, RICO has always provoked criticism from civil libertarians. When the use of RICO lawsuits became a popular weapon within the financial world, and money managers were facing RICO counts for alleged mishandling of their clients' investments, the criticism intensified. Even the Chief Justice of the Supreme Court, William Rehnquist, wrote an unusually blunt op-ed column in *The Wall Street Journal*, with the self-explanatory title: "Get RICO Cases Out of My Courtroom."

Late in the 1980s, the Rescuers who had devoted their lives to saving innocent babies found themselves classified alongside the gangsters who had earned profits by contract murders. They too were defendants in RICO cases. Chief Justice Rehnquist deplored that trend, too, but he ignored his first opportunity to halt it. In October 1989, Rehnquist and his colleagues had their first opportunity to review a RICO action against Operation Rescue. Michael McMonagle and twenty-six other defendants had been found guilty of criminal conspiracy, and faced over a hundred thousand dollars in fines, damages, and attorneys' fees. Although the essential purpose of RICO law is to punish criminal intent, the trial judge had prevented McMonagle and his fellow defendants from testifying about their motivation. Obviously the Rescuers had no hope of deriving financial profit from their actions. Yet the Third Circuit Appeals Court had rejected their protests, and now the U.S. Supreme Court refused to hear their case.

That decision sent abortionists scurrying back to consult with their lawyers again, and soon new RICO lawsuits were being filed. In Massachusetts, the Town of Brookline (home of three busy abortion mills) filed a RICO lawsuit, charging that twenty defendants had engaged in a criminal conspiracy, at a time when no court in Massachusetts had convicted any OR member on criminal charges. The Town of Brookline was ready and willing to equate Operation Rescue with a family of Mafia mobsters, but local prosecutors were not yet ready to prove that Rescuers were breaking the law. In Los Angeles Randall Terry had been charged with a felony conspiracy to commit a misdemeanor. In Brookline (a town he had never visited) he was accused of a criminal conspiracy to engage in an action which may or may not have been classified as a crime!

In West Hartford, Connecticut, Randall Terry was slapped with another RICO lawsuit. As evidence against him, the town cited his book *Operation Rescue*. Did that approach constitute an attack on freedom of the press? If so, the attack was repeated. John Spear, the editor of the Orange County (N.Y.) Post who had written a scathing editorial criticism of the West Hartford police, was also named as a RICO defendant. When the Town of Brookline entered its RICO suit, only one of the Boston-based defendants had not been arrested two or more times in clinic blockades. That single individual was the editor of the Catholic Archdiocesan newspaper (and the author of this deposition), who had harshly criticized Brookline police in his editorial columns and in public speaking appearances. Ordinarily, whenever a newspaper editor faces legal charges stemming from a controversial editorial position, he can count on the support of other editors, regardless of any political disagreements. But in these cases, the major media ignore the clear chilling effect of the RICO lawsuits.

10

What Next?

THE AUTUMN of 1991 found several Rescue leaders embarking on new and unfamiliar projects. The happiest news came from Joan Andrews. In October she quietly married a New Jersey native and longtime friend, Chris Bell. Does married life presage a more conventional career for the veteran pro-life crusader? Not likely. Mr. Bell is (to no one's surprise) a dedicated pro-life activist himself, who operates shelters for unwed mothers and their children.

Also in October, Rev. Patrick Mahoney returned to Wichita — the city where he was last seen with a toothbrush in his shirt pocket, heading off to jail at Judge Kelly's command. When Pastor Joseph Slovenic had returned to Wichita on October 4, he was promptly arrested by federal marshals and clapped back in jail. Once again, Judge Kelly insisted that OR leaders could not enter his city without paying a hundred-thousand-dollar "peace bond"; since he refused to pay, Slovenic was violating the terms of the judicial decree that had chased the OR leadership out of Wichita before Labor Day. But Slovenic had been jailed for just a week when the Tenth Circuit Court of Appeals issued a ruling in the case, voiding Judge Kelly's demand for the hundred-thousand-dollar bond. So Slovenic was free to leave jail, and Mahoney could enter Wichita with one moral victory under his belt and another in his sights.

Mahoney set his sights high. On October 19, he announced his candidacy for the Presidency of the United States. Although he had not voted for Democratic Party candidates in the last two elections, Mahoney declared himself as a contender for that party's nomination in 1992, in an effort to "recapture" an old constituency. Although he is a Protestant minister himself, Mahoney contends that Catholic Americans should form the backbone of the Democratic Party, as they did during the high-water mark of Franklin Roosevelt's New Deal. By articulating a strong moral platform based on Christian principles, he continued, the Democratic Party could not only cement its hold on the Catholic vote but also tap the enormous political resources of the Evangelical denominations.

Mahoney's quest for the White House may be quixotic, but it is not superficial. Far from running as a one-issue candidate, Mahoney laid out a full platform that included support for balanced federal budgets, limitations on the terms of elected officials, and a foreign policy promoting human rights for the Catholic minority in Northern Ireland. Still, the abortion issue certainly provides the dominant factor in Mahoney's appeal and even in his campaign strategy. Readily admitting that he cannot raise the funds that other candidates will enjoy, he recognizes that he will not be able to mount a large-scale media effort. On the other hand, he argues, his campaign can already tap into a grass-roots organizational network which no other candidate can match: the two hundred fifty thousand dedicated activists who have joined the Rescue movement. And Mahoney's own commitment to the Rescue movement is unaffected by his political ambitions; he will continue organizing Rescues even during his campaign.

While Joan Andrews entered matrimony and Patrick Mahoney entered politics, Randall Terry took his own first steps into a new world: the Vatican. In November, the graduate of Elim Bible Institute found himself in Rome addressing a conference sponsored by the Pontifical Council for the Family. "I'm tremendously encouraged to be here," he told the Catholic News Service, "and I think it's an implicit recognition of Rescue as a viable part of the pro-life movement." He explained the Rescue mission to Catholic delegates from around the world and distributed a hundred copies of his book *Operation Rescue*. But his mission to Rome had two other purposes as well.

First, Terry came to support a group of Catholic leaders who had come to ask for a clear Vatican statement rebuking the American Catholic politicians who support abortion. Joseph Scheidler, acting on behalf of several Catholic pro-life leaders (including Joan Andrews, William Cotter of OR-Boston, and Father Paul Marx of Human Life International), presented Pope John Paul II with a formal canonical petition seeking church action against twenty-seven American politicians, including such national figures as New York Governor Mario Cuomo and Massachusetts Senator Edward

Kennedy, for their "notorious acts and/or statements which enable, support or condone abortion."

Second, Terry came with his own personal message for Pope John Paul. In his short conversation with the spiritual leader of some one billion Catholics, Terry was seeking moral support for the Rescue movement. When he met the Pope, Terry presented him with three gifts: a copy of his book, an Operation Rescue T-shirt, and a private letter.

The book might never be opened. The T-shirt seems destined for a similar fate. (When he presented his gifts, Terry explained that a T-shirt might be useful to a tennis-lover. "Oh, I'm too old," the chuckling pontiff replied.) But Terry has high hopes for the letter.

At that November meeting, the theme for the Pontifical Council was the assault on the dignity of human life, most notably through abortion. One speaker after another emphasized the urgency of the struggle, and top Vatican officials wholeheartedly agreed. As the meeting concluded, the Council asked Pope John Paul to write an encyclical letter to the Catholic faithful worldwide, alerting them to the cultural warfare that is already in progress and calling for their active participation in the battle. The Pope agreed to that request. And as he sits down to work on the encyclical, the pontiff will have that letter from Randall Terry pleading for a clear statement of support of Operation Rescue.

Is it realistic to expect that Pope John Paul might endorse the Rescue movement? There are some intriguing precedents. Mother Teresa of Calcutta, whose thinking so closely matches that of the Pope, once wrote to Joan Andrews saying, "What you are doing is right." In 1987 the Vatican's top doctrinal expert, Cardinal Joseph Ratzinger, issued a statement applauding the moral witness of nonviolent tactics: "A movement of passive resistance to the legitimation of practices contrary to human life and dignity is beginning to make an ever sharper impression upon the moral conscience" The Pope himself, remember, has told pro-life leaders: "In these matters, I take Mahatma Gandhi as my mentor."

Pope John Paul may not explicitly endorse the Rescue movement, and an encyclical letter would almost certainly not mention a specific organization such as Operation Rescue. But even an implicit statement of approval, even any subtle indication of the

Pope's enthusiasm, would provide an enormous boost to a movement recruiting among America's fifty million Catholics.

Freshly back from Vatican, and "tremendously encouraged" by his reception there, Randall Terry could offer only one firm prediction about what the future might hold in store: "The Rescue movement will not go away until child-killing is crushed."

Each time the Rescue movement has scored a new breakthrough, Terry pointed out, the success has caught even OR leaders by surprise. Not even Terry himself foresaw the dramatic growth of the Rescue effort in Atlanta in 1988, or the stunning transformation of Wichita in the summer of 1991. These triumphs came as gifts from above, he believes: "God reserves them for himself as an act of providence." He would not speculate on how, or when, or where the next breakthrough would come — only that it would come.

While waiting and praying for the finger of the Holy Spirit to touch the movement again, Rescuers are continuing with their own practical plans, carrying their battle onto several new fronts.

• Operation Rescue is marshaling its resources to prepare for the 1992 campaign season; Terry's group will organize mass Rescues in New York and Houston, to coincide with the Democratic and Republican Party conventions.

• "Youth for America" Rescues, organized primarily by teenagers, have cropped up across the country from Atlanta, Georgia, to Santa Rosa, California. Brian Longworth, director of the campaign, asks youngsters to remember that they are survivors of the post-*Roe* war on unborn children, and they should join in the struggle to help others escape the slaughter. In Atlanta, one youth Rescue included the dramatic witness of 14-year-old Gianna Jessen, who had survived a saline abortion. She earned one "save" in July 1991 by shouting: "Please don't abort your child like my mom did to me." The woman who heard that plea continued on her way into the abortuary, but the words echoed in her mind, and she soon came back out to ask for help.

• In Milwaukee, an extraordinarily active and aggressive Rescue group first began staging three Rescues each week, along with pickets outside the homes of local abortionists. The Missionaries to the Preborn also found a way to frustrate Dr. Aleksander Jakubowski, a busy abortionist who commuted to a Milwaukee clinic from his home in Illinois. One day, when he made his usual stop for coffee at a tollway rest area, Jakubowski returned to find Rescuers chained to the axles of his Mercedes-Benz.

The Milwaukee group has also popularized a controversial new approach to stopping abortion: "imprecatory prayers" seeking God's direct intervention to stop the abortionists' trade. As Rev. Matt Trewhella explains, "imprecation means, quite simply, to invoke a curse or judgment." If that approach struck some Christians as harsh, Trewhella responds: "What do you think Jesus was teaching us to do when he taught us to wipe the dust off our feet from a town that wouldn't accept us?" Whatever theological debates their approach might have touched off, the Milwaukee Rescuers have seen eye-popping results. Within the space of six months, six different abortionists have abandoned their practice in the Milwaukee area, citing reasons of health (in one case, death), financial setbacks, or sheer exhaustion brought on by the constant Rescue presence.

● Outside Milwaukee, the nationwide network of Missionaries to the Preborn has represented a new crusade for Atlanta's Joseph Foreman. Recognizing that most Christians could not leave their family responsibilities to engage in full-time Rescue work, Foreman has sought to recruit a handful of dedicated men and women who would "lay down their lives and rescue preborn children *continually.*" Perhaps for one or two years, or maybe for a lifetime, these missionaries would organize Rescues whenever they were not actually imprisoned. To sustain them, Foreman has asked Christian congregations to provide financial support, just as they would support any other parish missionary outreach.

● On the legal front, the New Jersey case of *Alexander v. Loce* offers fascinating possibilities for the pro-life movement in general, and Rescue work in particular. Alex Loce, of Queens, New York, had begged his fiancee to spare their unborn child. When she spurned his pleas and made an appointment at an abortuary in Morristown, New Jersey, Loce sought a court restraining order. Rebuffed in that effort as well, the desperate young father recruited fourteen pro-life friends to help him stage a Rescue at the Morristown clinic. When the case came to trial, Judge Michael Noonan allowed Loce to invoke the necessity defense against trespass charges, pointing out that the defendant was the child's father and had exhausted all other remedies. Judge Noonan also allowed expert witnesses to testify in court, establishing that human life begins in the womb at the time of conception.

Finally, in a provocative opinion, Judge Noonan wrote: "I find, based upon the undisputed medical and scientific testimony, that the eight-week-old fetus in this case was a living person, a human being legally executed pursuant to the U.S. Supreme Court." Because abortion is legal, he continued, the defendants had "no justifiable excuse to trespass and attempt to prevent a legal act of abortion." Alex Loce and his lawyers immediately recognized the importance of that judicial finding, and appealed the decision, hoping to establish the humanity of the unborn child as a matter of record in a higher court. Superior Court Judge Reginald Stanton, upholding Loce's conviction, nevertheless told *The New York Times* that "he would be willing to attempt to make the finding when life begins under the proper circumstances." If American courts established the fact that human life begins at conception — and the medical evidence is conclusive — lawyers might have the tool they need to justify Rescue blockades.

While Rescuers and their lawyers looked for new tactical approaches to the streetside battle against abortion, other pro-life activists escalated their battle in the spiritual plane. Fasting, spiritual combat, and prayer vigils outside abortion mills became increasingly common and remarkably effective. In Brooklyn, Bishop Thomas Daily regularly led Catholics in a public recitation of the rosary outside one local abortuary. These efforts were entirely legal, and the vigils did not block access to the abortion clinic. Nevertheless, business at that clinic slumped noticeably.

And yet, despite all the new initiatives begun by pro-life activists, despite the months of public witness, despite all the suffering, despite all the stories of injustice and brutality, despite all the babies saved — despite all the tumultuous history of the upstart Rescue movement, one single dominant fact remains: the great majority of American Christians are still on the sidelines, watching the battle rather than joining in the active struggle to save human lives. Bill Cotter of OR-Boston draws a gloomy conclusion: "All the signs are that Rescue is going to be just a small Remnant."

If Cotter's pessimism proves more accurate than Terry's

optimism, and the Rescue movement sags beneath the combined weight of hostile judges and apathetic Christians, will the Rescue movement be a failure? Not at all. Again Rescuers can take comfort in the words of Mother Teresa: "God has not called me to be successful. He has only called me to be obedient."

11

The Judgment of History

A T THE peak of the Wichita "Summer of Mercy," when Randall Terry flew to Kennebunkport, Maine, President George Bush politely refused to meet with the Operation Rescue leader, choosing instead to issue a broad statement that "everybody ought to obey the law." Yet on that very same day, the President also told reporters at his summer home that he admired dissident activists within the crumbling Soviet empire, who were defying their government in obedience to the "higher law of liberty."

Who can say when a cause justifies defiance of the law? Who makes the final judgment on whether a cause is so urgent, and a situation so dire, that direct action is required, regardless of the cost? Who decides when the time for compromise has ended and the time for battle has begun?

The answers to all those questions lie in the hearts of ordinary citizens. If Operation Rescue can pierce through the armor of complacency and convention, pricking the conscience of the American people, then the movement's success is assured. If it cannot reach out beyond a small band of pro-life militants, its failure is inevitable.

Operation Rescue is not one more political movement. Asked how he would classify his own work, Randall Terry does not describe himself as a political organizer or a pro-life activist, but as "a reformer who fears God." To be successful, the movement he leads must help to instill that same fear of God in thousands of other American Christians.

Pro-life work is not the only form of Christian service. God-fearing Americans have innumerable, different public tasks before them: feeding the poor, strengthening the family, counseling the troubled, in general restoring the primacy of God in American culture. And none of those tasks can be accomplished unless individual Christians nourish the development of their own spiritual lives. Still, when the clash between moral good and evil is as clear and decisive as it is in the abortion industry — when death confronts life thousands of time every day — no Christian can ignore the struggle.

In Operation Rescue, Terry explains his reasoning with a quotation from Martin Luther: "If I profess with the loudest voice and the clearest exposition every portion of the truth of God except precisely that little point which the world and the devil are at the moment attacking, I am not confessing Christ, however boldly I may be professing Christ. Where the battle rages, there the loyalty of the soldier is proved, and to be steady on all the battlefield besides is mere flight and disgrace if he flinches at that point."

Terry readily embraces that military metaphor. During one prison term, he spent his spare time reading the thoughts of the ancient Chinese philosopher Lao Tse on the art of warfare, explaining simply that he too was at war. He characterizes America's current turmoil as a civil war, a "battle for cultural dominance," in which "there will only be one winner."

Can he win?

As the year 1991 drew toward a close, OR could claim to represent at most two hundred fifty thousand Americans — roughly one-tenth of one percent of the American population. It is, by any rational political measurement, a tiny minority. But a bit of perspective is necessary here. Five years ago, the Rescue movement could not claim even five thousand active supporters. If it remains at the current level, politicians can safely dismiss the Rescue movement. If it continues to grow at its current pace, the Rescue movement will revolutionize American politics before the year 2000.

To no one's surprise, Randall Terry contends that the movement will continue its explosive growth. The final victory will not come immediately, he admitted to a *Time* magazine reporter. Still his timetable was breathtakingly ambitious: "The pollution and degradation of this culture did not happen overnight, and neither will our ability to reclaim it and reform it happen overnight. It's going to take a good half-generation to turn things around."

A half-generation? Can the Rescue movement rout the entrenched interests of the abortion culture in the space of a decade? Terry fervently believes so. He reminds audiences of Christ's promise that "the gates of Hell shall not prevail" against the Church.

Gates, he points out, are weapons of defense, not offense. The Lord's guarantee applies when Christians take the battle into the enemy's camp. When the Church is mobilized, and Christians seize the offensive in the struggle for cultural dominance, they will soon overwhelm the bastions of the abortion industry — and sweep out a host of moral evils in their path.

The image is vivid, and Terry's preaching conveys an infectious energy. But again, is it realistic?

There are precedents. In 1850 the Abolitionist movement was a tiny minority outside the mainstream of American politics, occupying a niche similar to the one filled by Operation Rescue today. But that was also the year when the Abolitionist Theodore Parker, defying the Fugitive Slave Law, led a group into a Boston courtroom and forcibly freed a fugitive, proclaiming it the "noblest deed done in Boston since the destruction of the tea." Parker's eloquent action excited the sympathies of powerful "mainstream" politicians like Charles Sumner and Horace Mann, and the Abolitionist movement vaulted onto an entirely different political plane. Within months slavery was the single issue dominating American politics, and soon — in the space of "a good half-generation" — Abraham Lincoln had signed the Emancipation Proclamation, and the culture of slavery was overthrown.

A century later, the civil-rights activists of the Southern Christian Leadership Conference carefully chose Selma, Alabama, as the site for a 1965 protest. Martin Luther King and his colleagues predicted that a violent response from Selma's Sheriff Jimmy Clark would guarantee broad exposure for their cause. In *Protest at Selma* (Yale Universsity Press, 1978) David Garrow explains: "King accurately believed that nothing could be more effective in activating support among the national audience for the movement and its goals than scenes of peaceful demonstrators, seeking their birthright as American citizens, being violently attacked." Sure enough, on March 7 — "Bloody Sunday" — the ABC television network interrupted its evening broadcast to show shocking footage from Pettus Bridge, outside Selma, where police were brutally clubbing the civil-rights activists. By the end of that year, the civil-rights activists were celebrating another momentous victory: the passage of the Voting Rights Act.

Could one of the sidewalk confrontations provoked by OR — this year, or next year, or even several years from now — become the same sort of flashpoint, igniting a massive burst of pro-life activism? Or has that crucial turning point already come, undetected by contemporary historians, in Atlanta or West Hartford or Wichita?

In early August 1991, *The Wichita Eagle* and a local television station, KAKE-TV, co-sponsored a poll to measure the city's response to the OR campaign. An overwhelming seventy-eight-percent majority expressed disapproval for the Rescuers' methods. Abortion-rights activists promptly proclaimed a public-relations victory.

But wait. During the heyday of the civil-rights movement, pollsters had found a similar majority disapproving of the protestors. After the 1963 protest marches in Birmingham, a Gallup poll found sixty percent of all respondents complaining that such demonstrations would set back the cause of the civil-rights movement. Yet within months those marchers had attained their main objective: the passage of the Civil Rights Act. In 1965 most Americans would still have assessed Martin Luther King a large share of the blame for the bloodshed on Pettus Bridge, yet the Voting Rights Act followed. Could OR enjoy the same ultimate success?

Consider that poll result from a different angle. While 78% disapproved of OR, 12% strongly approved. In a city such as Wichita, with a population of over 350,000, that 12% figure suggests 40,000 people — all strongly approving the effort to close down the abortuaries by nonviolent protest. If OR can ever mobilize even a substantial fraction of that number — in Wichita or any other American city — the abortion industry is doomed.

How could the Rescue movement possibly gather forty thousand people outside the clinic doors — especially in the face of a frightening federal injunction? Most ordinary people cannot face the threat of jail. Even devout Christians have families to raise, bills to pay, homes and possessions to protect from lawsuits. How can the great mass of ordinary American Christians join in the battle, alongside the handful of activists who have devoted their lives to the cause?

Preaching at Rescue rallies, Joseph Foreman offers an answer to those questions, based on the Old Testament book of Numbers.

("How many people here have read Numbers recently," he asks the audience. Receiving the blank response he expected, he cracks, "The trouble with you people is that you haven't done enough jail time.") His text is the thirty-second chapter of Numbers. As Moses is marshaling the forces of Israel for the final entry into the Promised Land, after forty years of painful wandering in the desert, two of the twelve tribes of Israel — the Reubenites and Gadites — announce that they would prefer to remain in the fertile area across the Jordan. Their families are comfortable there, the leaders of those two tribes explain, and their herds of livestock are flourishing on the land that Israel already controls. They feel no need for another conquest.

Moses rebukes the Reubenites and Gadites: "Do you intend your brothers to go into battle while you stay here?" But they soon offer a compromise. If Moses will allow them time to settle their families, to "build sheepfolds here for our flocks and towns for our little ones," then they will join Israel in the battle for Canaan, and "We will not return to our homes until every one of the Israelites has taken possession of his heritage."

That is a reasonable request, Foreman notes, and Moses promptly grants it. But even as he grants the request, Moses offers a stern warning (Num 32:20-22):

> "If you do as you have said, if you are prepared to fight before Yahweh, and if all those of you who bear arms cross the Jordan before Yahweh, until he has driven all his enemies out before him, then, once the country has become subject to Yahweh, you may go back, and will have discharged your obligation to Yahweh and Israel, and Yahweh will consider this territory yours. But if you do not, you will sin against Yahweh, and be sure your sins will find you out."

That same stern injunction could apply to American Christians today, Foreman tells his audience. Most have obligations to uphold, and commitments that prevent them from joining wholeheartedly in the battle to protect life. Their position is entirely understandable; their obligations are both serious and just.

But Foreman counsels those ordinary Americans to look seriously at all their obligations and follow the advice Moses set out

for the Reubenites and Gadites. Discharge those obligations, he
exhorts his audience. Pay off those debts; finish that education;
educate those children; complete that project. Above all, break all the
habits of self-indulgence that prevent Christians from devoting
themselves fully to the Lord's work.

Finally, Foreman counsels the quiet Christian majority, set a
timetable. Will it take two years to settle all those obligations, to
remove all those impediments, to be ready at last to join in the battle?
Fine. Set a schedule, work on it, eliminate the obstacles, and when
the time comes, enlist in the cause. Might that process require five
years? That, too, is fine. The length of time is not crucial; the
important point is to make a commitment and stick to it. "But if you
do not, you will sin against Yahweh, and be sure your sins will find
you out."

Foreman ends his plea with an appeal that captures the essence
of the Rescue movement's challenge to the American conscience.
Not every Christian is called to join the Rescue movement, he
admits, but every loyal Christian must do something to stop the
slaughter. Will the struggle be difficult? Yes. But to follow Christ
means to share the burden that Jesus took to Calvary. Not every
Christian is called to join the blockade lines, but every Christian is
surely called to join in the struggle. Participation in Operation
Rescue is not the only measure of Christian witness, Foreman
concludes: "That might not be the cross God wants you to carry. But
I guarantee you this: God wants you to carry a cross."

Appendix 1: For Further Information

A LTHOUGH THE mainstream media rarely provide accurate information about the Rescue movement, interested readers can readily find ways to keep abreast of the latest developments.

Operation Rescue-National produces a newsletter for interested parties as often as the group's finances permit. The new address for OR-National — which has moved since the bulk of this book was completed — is P.O. Box 127, Summerville, SC 29484. Many local Rescue groups also publish their own newsletters, covering efforts in their particular geographic areas. Anyone who attends Rescue rallies — or even more general pro-life gatherings — will find literature available from a host of smaller local, regional, and nationwide groups.

The best and broadest single source of Rescue news is *Life Advocate*, a fine monthly newsmagazine devoted specifically to the Rescue movement. Although *Life Advocate* devotes extra attention to developments in the Pacific Northwest, where the magazine is published, the news coverage extends all across the country and embraces many different groups within the Rescue movement. There is no set subscription price, but readers are asked to send a contribution to: *Life Advocate*, P.O. Box 13656, Portland, OR 97213.

Appendix 2: Mini-Bibliography

SIX EXCELLENT books, all readily available in Christian bookstores, will provide more insight into the history and thought of the Rescue movement (author or editor, title, publisher, city, date):

Randy Alcorn, *Is Rescuing Right?* (InterVarsity Press, Madison Wis., 1990)
A thorough and balanced analysis of the relevant scriptural passages, written principally for an Evangelical Christian audience, concludes that the Rescue movement is on solid theological ground.

Joan Andrews, with John Cavanaugh-O'Keefe, *I Will Never Forget You: The Rescue Movement in the Life of Joan Andrews* (Ignatius Press, San Francisco, 1989)
An autobiographical look at the movement through the eyes of its most celebrated practitioner.

Richard Cowden-Guido (editor), *You Reject Them, You Reject Me: The Prison Letters of Joan Andrews* (Trinity Communications, Manassas, Va., 1988)
Read this eccentric collection of letters from, to, and about the imprisoned "St. Joan," and you will understand how she acquired that nickname.

Joseph Scheidler, *Closed: 99 Ways to Stop Abortion* (Regnery Books, Regnery-Gateway, Inc., Washington, D.C., 1985)
For years *the* standard operating manual for pro-life activists, laced with the tactical wisdom of a sidewalk veteran.

Randall Terry, *Operation Rescue* (Whitaker House, Springdale, Pa., 1988)

Written from inside a jail cell, this book offers the first complete expression of the OR vision, from the man whose leadership thrust the Rescue movement onto the headlines and into the nation's conscience.

Randall Terry, *Accessory to Murder* (Wolgemuth & Hyatt, Brentwood, Tenn., 1990)

With righteous indignation buttressed by solid research, Terry explains how many of our society's institutions — the media, the courts, legislatures, and even churches — have made their peace with the abortion culture.

Appendix 3: Acknowledgments

TWO CHAPTERS of this book have appeared, in slightly different form, in monthly publications. Chapter Two appeared in the October 1991 issue of *Catholic World Report*, and Chapter Nine appeared in the March 1992 issue of *Crisis*. I am grateful to the editors of both magazines.

This book could not have appeared without the support — moral and material — provided by Bob Lockwood, publisher of *Our Sunday Visitor* and president of OSV, Inc. My research was aided tremendously by Operation Rescue-Boston and its leader, Bill Cotter; Mary Schumacher and Bob Delery were also helpful.

My classmate John Cavanaugh-O'Keefe was the man whose unsettling arguments forced me to take the Rescue movement seriously. When I finally joined, and paid the price, he was prompt to offer his support. During the same difficult period I was profoundly grateful for the outpouring of support and encouragement I received — and still receive — from my friends and fellow Rescuers in the Boston area.

Dr. Joe Stanton, whose moving "Letter From Brookline Jail" is included here as an appendix, has frequently given me access to the two most valuable archives available to the American pro-life movement. The *second* most valuable archive can be found in his crowded Dickensian offices at the Value of Life Committee. The *most* valuable archive resides between Dr. Stanton's ears.

Dozens of Rescuers helped me with my research, and dozens more offered their support, but several deserve special recognition. Randall Terry crawled out of a sickbed to answer some last-minute questions as my deadline pressed upon me. Chris Slattery and Pat Monaghan — my brothers in different enterprises — were particularly generous with their explanations, advice, and encouragement.

Accepting one cup of coffee as payment for his legal services, Frank McNamara defended me against RICO charges, then patiently answered my questions when I became lost in the thicket of courtroom technicalities that often arise in Rescue cases.

Most of the photographs contained in this book, including the cover photo, are reprinted here through the courtesy of Operation Rescue-Boston (with a special nod of thanks to photographer Dale O'Leary) and of *Life Advocate* magazine.

As always, my best friend, critic, promoter, editor, agent, comforter, and adviser (not to mention proofreader) was my wife Leila. She and our six children have made many more sacrifices than I have, without a second thought, and always sustained me with their prayers.

Appendix 4: Letter From Brookline Jail

(The following essay, a classic document in the history of Operation Rescue, was written on paper towels in a Brookline, Mass., jail's holding cell in March 1989 by Dr. Joseph Stanton, a pioneer in the right-to-life movement.)

To our fellow citizens, Peace!

In eerie stillness, broken only by occasional cough or restless stirring, it is three A.M. The outside street lights diffracted through the two small opaque windows of the holding area at the Police Station on Washington Street, Brookline, have tricked an aging body, even now emerging from restless sleep, into believing that it must be close to seven A.M. this third day of confinement, and that time when we begin to prepare for our appearance in court! Strewn about me, covering almost every square inch of the floor of the holding area, lie the sleeping bodies of sixty of my brothers in the Lord. Scattered through the other holding facilities of the Brookline Police Department this night are some hundred other, previously law-abiding, men and women.

Called to the higher mandate of Proverbs 24:11 to "Rescue those being dragged to death," at 7:45 A.M., Saturday, March 5, we stood or sat on sidewalk and street in front of the three abortion clinics on Beacon Street, Brookline, and refused to move. For interposing our bodies between wholly innocent unborn children in the womb and the abortionist, over two hundred of us have been arrested and handcuffed, carried or dragged to police wagon or bus, transported under guard through the streets of this town, photographed and fingerprinted as lawbreakers, and confined.

Allowed the criminal's one official phone call to relative or lawyer, with serenity — even joy — in solidarity and fellowship in the Lord of life and death, we willingly accept whatever judgment or deprivation is the verdict of a society which treats as legal and respectable the slaughter of four thousand unborn children each day. As we have sung hopefully so many times, "They will know we are Christians by our love." That love encompasses each of our fellow citizens, born or unborn, the police who see it as their duty to arrest and confine us, the abortionists and abortion advocates, and very poignantly the troubled woman and girl for whom an uncaring society portrays the taking of the life of her unborn child as a "right," not a grave moral wrong.

We, over two hundred arrestees, are male and female. We are black and white, clergyman and seminary student, housewife, husband, mother and father, grandfather and grandmother, postal worker, teacher, nun, student. We range in age from 16 to a great-grandmotherly young 76. We assemble from across Greater Boston and New England to as far away as New York.

We have found that the biblical mandate from Proverbs to "Rescue those being dragged to death" does not cut the mustard these days in the Town of Brookline. Displayed on the bulletin board in the holding room where I write these lines is a letter signed by Jeffrey Allen, Chairman of the Board of Selectmen. He congratulates the police force for their expeditious "handling" of the prior Operation Rescue and offering to buy whatever additional equipment is necessary "to keep the abortion clinics open." We, the enemy, are described as "those people." I am told that he has said in an interview that the town has had to spend money on "blankets and food." For the two peanut butter and jelly sandwiches and two McDonald hamburgers which have sustained this body these last forty-eight hours, I am grateful to God, Mr. Allen, and the Selectmen. But if (as the *Globe* reported) money was expended for blankets for us, no detainees have seen pillow or blanket or bed. The floor is our bed and small red ants our companions.

Many abortions were not done in Brookline on Saturday morning. In the larger sense, one can ask if this action — deliberately breaking the law, putting stress on society, its police, its Board of Selectmen — by those who across a lifetime *always* respected and obeyed the law, is defensible? Many of us arrested Saturday have for almost two decades now, working within the law, sought to reverse the constitutionally indefensible *Roe* and *Doe* decisions. We have experienced what Senator James Buckley of

New York said in the Congressional Record for the Senate on May 31, 1973: "The issue at stake is not only what we do to unborn children but what we do to ourselves by permitting them to be killed. With every day that passes, we run the danger of stumbling willy-nilly down the path that leads inexorably to the devaluation of all stages of human life born and unborn."

At this moment, in our society, Planned Parenthood and other powerful abortion purveyors are spending hundreds of thousands of dollars for coathanger advertisements and the most skillful products of Madison Avenue to try to influence our fellow citizens of the abortion "right." Those of us privileged to oppose the taking of innocent human life do not have their financial resources. We have only our bodies and our freedom, which we cherish, which we willingly offer up in act of love to the Lord, God of life, and as a plea for our unborn brothers and sisters. For one who accepts personally as his own Francis Thompson's self-assessment in "The Hound of Heaven," this "of all earth's clotted clay thou dingiest clot," after sixty-eight privileged years, sees in a willingness to suffer the privations of jail, in offering this body to protect an unborn child, virtue and loving commitment.

In this jail, one who has so often and so futilely and so petulantly worried about the future found peace. When those of us long in the saddle falter or fall, I have worried, where will the new warriors come from to sustain this awesome battle for the soul of a nation? In the more than two hundred brothers and sisters in the Lord who were arrested with me, and other Operation Rescue volunteers in other jails this night, my trepidations have vanished. I have sensed as never before the contours of a powerful force of profound commitment and depth of purpose and dedication. In the biblical sense, we are a mighty army in the Lord. The days of *Roe v. Wade* and *Doe v. Bolton* are numbered. No longer is it a question of *if*; it is only a question of *when* they will pass into the dustbins of history along with the Herodian slaughter of the innocents.

You may find our deliberate actions embarrassing and inconvenient. You may wish that we would go away. But such will not be. No temporal power, no press, no flailing of Planned Parenthood can extinguish the fire, ignited now and burning ever more brightly in the soul of this nation as I write. Not everyone is called upon to be willing to go to jail, but each of us is called upon to pray to recognize the sacredness of each human life formed by Him. "Even if your mother would forget you, I will never forget you. See, I have carved your name on the palm of my hand" (Isaiah 49:15-16). Recognition of this mystery and the fact that each one of us was redeemed in His blood and the burden it lays on each of us, once grasped, is the source of the power of Operation Rescue.

My brothers and sisters in the Lord, each member of Operation Rescue in jail this night, like Sts. Peter and Paul, and Thomas More and Maximilian Kolbe, and Mahatma Gandhi, and Martin Luther King, is empowered and imprisoned for acting on our beliefs. We seek your understanding and we offer you our love.

— JOSEPH R. STANTON, M.D.
 Brookline, Mass., March 7, 1989

Appendix 5: 'What's a Nice Girl Like You . . ?'

The following piece by John Mallon, now of Steubenville, Ohio, but then a student at Boston College, appeared on the Op-Ed page of the March 31, 1989, issue of The Pilot, *weekly newspaper of the Archdiocese of Boston.*

ONE OF the few remaining places where a single Catholic male can meet a nice Cathol'c girl these days is in jail. After being on the sidewalk blocking the entrance to an abortion mill. You can pretty well assume that she takes her faith — and The Faith — seriously and probably doesn't scoff at things like virginity, purity, chastity, and love, or view motherhood as a male plot to oppress women. She will know what she believes — and why — perhaps from bitter experience. She will have a light shining through her. Pro-life women may be the last hope for American womanhood.

These are the people our society is starting to arrest these days. It is hard to meet such a woman at the Catholic universities, which have no shortage of pro-abortion feminists, and others hell-bent on liberating women from the "oppressive" shackles of Catholicism into the freedom of being "sexually active" — complete with the right to prevent or dispose of any possible results from that activity.

With the assault on femininity in full force, what is a simple Catholic boy to do in his search for female companionship except to join the fight for the restoration of womanhood (among other things) by stopping the socially sanctioned killing of babies? What else, but get in the way of law-abiding folks who kill babies for a living? Try to rescue the women and children who will suffer from this legalized carnage.

Could the pro-life movement be the last bastion of feminine loveliness and strength? Young, male, Christian friends of mine have commented to me on the lovely qualities and virtue of the women they meet at Operation Rescue demonstrations. This is not to trivialize the solemn business of saving children from death and their mothers from trauma. These young men are absolutely committed to the cause; like the two Boston College students I saw throw themselves in front of a moving bus full of pro-life prisoners to buy time for the babies. Where else can you find that level of Christian community, commitment, and fellowship these days? It is even ecumenical.

It cannot be ignored that modernism's all-out assault on love, family, femininity, masculinity, womanhood, manhood, motherhood, fatherhood, sex, child conceiving, bearing, and rearing has necessarily played havoc with youthful romance. And it is indeed about the business of banishing romance down the same road that it has already driven genteel courtship. What The World takes for romance is really seduction — a race to bed rather than a gentle dance of mutual discovery. A good woman is as hard to find as a good man used to be — a good man perhaps even harder than ever.

Catholics who have received the grace of being set in their vocations and lives are sometimes uncomfortable with young, single Catholics; and frequently have a well-meaning impulse to prod them into a seminary or convent, or marry them off. It is not so simple anymore. For all the concern over the shortage of priests and religious, what is often missed is the fact that the vocation crisis cuts across all vocations. There don't seem to be very many people getting married these days, either. The vocation crisis is across the board. It is a crisis of commitment, but it is not the fault of the young. Having grown up with divorce, religious dissent, and "shifting values," most of them don't know what commitment *looks like*.

Imagine yourself to be eighteen, today. In high school it is drugs, in college it is drunkenness and sex. At a Catholic college the implied spiritual message is that it doesn't matter what you do, as long as you are "nice" — and use a condom. It isn't nice to "oppress" students with moral guidelines; they might leave the Church. The upshot is that the students can be like their dissenting teachers: they can leave the Church and think they are in it at the same time. The only student marginalized at the Catholic university is the faithful Catholic seeking to live a Godly life while thinking with the Church. But, of course, that's what they get for being so "backward, narrow-minded, and conservative." It is not easy. But the good news is that, in such an atmosphere, despite — or perhaps because of —the opposition, some young saints are being raised up by God and attaining heroic sanctity just by being who they are, in Christ, in a hostile environment. It is ironic: Fostering sanctity is one thing Catholic universities were created for, yet are they supposed to succeed in such a roundabout way?

Well . . . God always has the last laugh. While the heterodox dissenters cry "oppression" ceaselessly, it is the orthodox student who is oppressed and isolated.

So where can you go to meet a good and faithful young Catholic man or woman in this day and age? In jail. Where else?

* * *

If God shall grant me the gift of someday having children and the grace to live to see my children's children, I will proudly recall and tell them of the times I lived in, especially the day four Brookline policemen picked me up, hands bound, and carried me, exultant with a joy that could only have come from God, and threw me into a patrol wagon where I looked up to find I had landed at the feet of Dr. Joseph Stanton.

In an age where a Catholic university theology faculty and a chaplain publicly defend and condone birth control and abortion counseling on a Catholic campus to a national Catholic publication, while their undergraduate (and graduate) students from that same university are going to jail in defense of life, and finding more joy and friendship in jail than they do on campus, something is seriously wrong. Someone is trying to tell us something. And maybe it's God.

I am intensely proud to be of the flock of an archdiocese where the editor of my archdiocesan paper places himself and his freedom on the line in a personal decision to save babies. (I know you will wince at printing this, Phil, but don't you dare edit a word.)

A recent *Pilot* headline read: "Pope calls for greater lay activism." The secular press reports the Vatican summoning the American bishops to Rome to toughen up and be martyrs for the Faith if necessary. In light of this, I hope that our Archbishop could hold his head high and report to the Holy Father that, as they spoke,

153

some two hundred of his flock, along with other faithful Christians, were in jail for Christ — in America.

Dr. Stanton's "Letter From Brookline Jail" (*Pilot* 3/10/89) is surely an instant classic in the literature of the pro-life movement. We have here a man of medicine who must go to jail in order to help heal an ailing nation. We have college students giving Christian witness to those charged with giving them formation but who instead, in apparent despair, accommodate evil. We have a Catholic editor pushed by conscience into a position of *being* news instead of just reporting it. The Archdiocese of Boston can be extremely grateful and proud. Glory be to God.

— JOHN MALLON
Brighton, Mass.